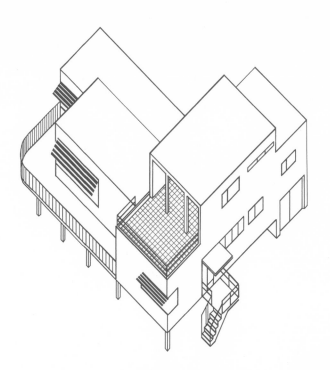

STYLISTIC
COLD WARS

TIMOTHY MOWL

STYLISTIC COLD WARS

VERSUS

JOHN MURRAY
Albemarle Street, London

Endpapers: A drawing by John Piper to illustrate a *Murray's Guide*;
and a Modern Movement house, drawn by Dan Plotkin

First published in 2000
by John Murray (Publishers) Ltd,
50 Albemarle Street, London W1X 4BD

ISBN 0-7195-5909 X

Typeset in 12/13 Monotype Walbaum by Servis Filmsetting Ltd
Printed and bound in Great Britain by The University Press,
Cambridge

Contents

Acknowledgements

MY THANKS GO first of all to Dieter and Uta Pevsner and to Dieter's son, Mark, for family reminiscences of Nikolaus both at Hampstead and in Wiltshire, then to Virginia Murray, the archivist at Albemarle Street, for her kindness and enthusiasm as I worked through the Jock Murray–John Betjeman papers. I have not met Betjeman's daughter, Candida Lycett Green, but we have exchanged letters, and the three volumes of her father's correspondence and his prose, which she has edited, have been my constant reference works for the last year. Similarly I should like to acknowledge Bevis Hillier for his *Young Betjeman*. John R. Murray, who edited Betjeman's last books and knew the poet well, has corrected me on several misapprehensions.

I should also like to thank all those friends, colleagues and correspondents who have drawn my attention to caches of letters and useful printed texts. David Watkin was kind enough to entertain me one afternoon in Albany with his forthright views on both Betjeman and Pevsner. It was his book, *Morality and Architecture*, which originally alerted me to the central problems discussed here. Others who have been particularly helpful include Ruth Guilding and Andrew Wilson, Geoffrey Beard, Alan Powers, Dan Cruickshank, Andrew Mead, John Harris, Simon Richards, Brian Earnshaw, Luke Gasparo, Patrick Bryan, Kit Wedd, Steven Parissien and Gordon Kelsey.

Of the various archivists I have consulted I should like to

Acknowledgements

make special mention of Christine Penney at Birmingham University who helped unravel Pevsner's early days in England; Nicholas Lee, Michael Richardson and Hannah Lowery at Bristol University who guided me through the Allen Lane archive there; and Anthony Beeson at Bristol Public Library. Simon Bradley at *The Buildings of England* was most helpful over the *Pevsner* guides and Richard Holder at the Victorian Society answered my queries about the early days of that amenity society.

My thanks to my editorial team at John Murray — Caroline Knox, Grant McIntyre, Gail Pirkis and Stephanie Allen — for their continued professionalism with this, my third book for them. Thanks also to Douglas Matthews for compiling the index. My agent, Sara Menguc, has never doubted that this was a subject worth pursuing and I am grateful for her reassurance at a critical time in the writing. During our trips of despair to watch Bristol City, my son Adam was always encouraging as our attention understandably drifted from the action on the pitch to our ongoing projects. Finally I must thank my wife, Sarah, for her unfailing support and for introducing me to that stretch of North Cornwall around the Camel estuary to which Betjeman always returned and where we now take our annual holiday.

TIMOTHY MOWL
Bristol
Spring 1999

ILLUSTRATIONS
The photograph of John Betjeman on p. ix was taken by Jock Murray in the summer of 1956 and is reproduced courtesy of the John Murray Archive. That of Nikolaus Pevsner on p. viii, taken in 1973 by Frank Hermann, is reproduced courtesy of the Allen Lane Archive at the University of Bristol.

The photographs of Pevsner's grave at Clyffe Pypard (p. 171) and that of Betjeman in St Enodoc churchyard (p. 170) were taken by the author.

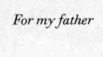

For my father

INTRODUCTION

One Chalk Cliff, One Poet and One Architectural Historian

There is a long green chalk cliff where the Marlborough Downs rise abruptly, some 300 feet above the Vale of the White Horse and the flat country of the Thames valley. The escarpment extends across two counties, Berkshire and Wiltshire, with a whole string of villages lying at its foot: Compton Bassett, Clevancy, Clyffe Pypard, Broad Town and Wroughton in Wiltshire, and Ashbury, Compton Beauchamp, Woolstone and Uffington in Berkshire. They offer that mildly dramatic rural individuality that London weekenders prize. The poet and critic Geoffrey Grigson, who seems to have spent his adult life sampling atmospheric environments everywhere in Britain, lived in Broad Town for a while, writing appreciatively of 'the strangest light effects' that could be enjoyed there from the cliff's morning shadow and its evening reflections. The views out to the north have been compared with Rubens's major landscape studies and they certainly do have that same Flemish breadth of focus.

Coincidentally John Betjeman and Nikolaus Pevsner both had houses within a few miles of each other in the lee of this wave of downland. I write 'coincidentally' because there is, after all, only a finite range of characterful rural bolt-holes for urbanites. But the more the careers of the two men are pursued the more parallel and yet antithetical to each other they seem to be.

1

Introduction

A coincidental choice of houses on the edge of Wessex down-land should not be pressed too far, but it is mildly odd that two such inimical – even, from Betjeman's side, hostile – characters should have been drawn to the same idiosyncratic fold of land, just as they were drawn together, time and again, to serve on the committees and august bodies that advise and inform the British state on architectural aesthetics.

Over the middle years of the century, from 1950 onwards and well into the 1970s, these two men, Pevsner the academic, lecturer and codifier, Betjeman the poet, journalist and media manipulator, exercised more influence over architectural taste than any trained architect or government minister. Pevsner's *Buildings of England*, all forty-six volumes, had made him the natural authority, consulted and deferred to, in most cases where historic structures were under threat. Betjeman was the television celebrity, the unpretentious aesthete and, after 1972, the Poet Laureate. To him preservation societies turned automatically for support when the demolition men and the developers were closing in on well-loved landmarks of town, village or countryside. Both men were arbiters of taste to a visually under-educated nation, yet they never, despite appearances, worked together in any friendly accord or mutual respect. They held entirely contrary views on style and on how the country should be building. In their two persons the national dilemma of direction was summed up but never openly expressed.

Nikolaus Pevsner, being German-born, preserved the caution of an *émigré* in his adopted country. Whatever his private opinion of John Betjeman's scholarship he maintained a courteous reserve and passed no judgements. Working steadily through the English counties, recording 'every building of architectural significance', he saw it as his business to record facts and banish obscurities. But obscurities were what Betjeman, the romantic, relished most. The nineteenth century was a period of particular interest to both Pevsner and Betjeman but, as Sir John Summerson observed in a lecture to the PEN Club, for Betjeman 'the twilight which had settled on the

Victorian and Edwardian was a beautiful, tragical-comical twilight. It was not an academic problem looking for an academic answer. Hence his antagonism towards Pevsner, which for a time was obsessional.' There was antagonism and yet there was this shared feeling for the same reach of downland. It is as if, after very different early years, they came to shadow each other, with Pevsner's achievement a commentary upon Betjeman's, or even a mockery of it.

In 1934, soon after their marriage and some unfortunate experience of London flats, the Betjemans – John and Penelope – rented Garrards Farm, a large limewashed clunch house with bold brick window surrounds, set in Uffington village, immediately below the sleekly stylized, prehistoric White Horse. Betjeman painted his own rude murals over the dining-room mantelpiece – a naked lady with tulips – the furnishings were Arts and Crafts, the curtains Voysey-patterned, and here they entertained informally and often. It was a happy house and they only left in 1945 because the farmer wanted it for his son. Then, in 1951, after six years at the Old Rectory in Farnborough, the highest and coldest village in Berkshire, they moved down to live under the cliff again in Wantage.

Pevsner came to the area later. In 1946, after using it intermittently as a holiday refuge during the war years, he bought Geoffrey Grigson's small, and initially rather squalid, herdsman's cottage, two up and two down, a damp, crumbling clunch structure clinging to that abrupt slope above Little Town Farm, east of Broad Town where Grigson had retired to enjoy electricity and mains water. Betjeman's Garrards Farm stands right in the village with extensive farm buildings which housed Penelope Betjeman's white Arab gelding, Moti, and her goats. Pevsner's Hardyesque hovel is at the end of a three-quarter-mile farm track, its last stretches rutted and unpaved. A watercourse, dry for most of the year, runs down steeply between the cottage and a shadowing yew tree where a patch of cyclamen of Grigson's planting still flowers. Two acres of the cliff, bought along with the house, all for £40 in those days of post-war property bargains, are covered with a rough scrub of hawthorn, wayfaring tree, bramble and old man's beard, and three little wooden huts perch in clearings.

The Pevsners were and remain a close family. Nikolaus and Lola had a daughter, Uta, and two boys, Dieter and Tomas. All three married and have three children each, so with nine grandchildren coming to spend holidays in the cottage those two cramped upstairs bedrooms were quite inadequate. An extension was added in the 1970s in roughly the same style as the original, in no way high-tech or modernist; but for reunions of the clan the wooden huts are still needed. It was in the earliest of these frail structures that Pevsner wrote the introductions to his *Buildings of England* guides, though the hut seems unlikely to survive long enough for either a preservation order or a blue plaque. Next to the Pevsners' scrub jungle is a bare, headlong field where another white horse has been carved into the turf. It is a simple nursery outline, much smaller than its Uffington relative. Pevsner once paid to have it scoured and weeded. In his *Wiltshire* volume it is given a modest mention with the date, 1863.

The cottage, originally called 'Under the Cliff' but now rechristened 'Snowhill', has never been more than the Pevsners' Wiltshire *gîte*. One of Nikolaus's grandsons, Mark, an administrator based in Luxemburg, was there with his wife Judith and young family when I visited. He and his father Dieter have happy memories of those earlier, more austere, days when they would all put their bicycles on the train at Paddington, get out at Wootton Bassett station and pedal their way to a cottage of oil lamps, laboriously pumped water and cold bedrooms. One senses, or perhaps this is a case of reading back the popular image of Nikolaus Pevsner's aesthetics, that the Spartan conditions of Snowhill cottage and that wooden writing hut were the essence of their charm. For all that, Pevsner tends to be remembered as a typical Hampstead resident and his three children still live on the Heath in what they call the 'Pevsner Gulag'; Uta in her father's Victorian Wildwood Terrace of stock brick with an angular polychromatic brick trim, Dieter in the earlier, post-Regency Wildwood Grove below it. But Pevsner in his prime was a country walker, tall, broad-shouldered, quietly spoken, one of the Wandervögel transferred from the forests of the Erz Gebirge to walk the Wiltshire downs. At heart he was Wordsworthian and at Snowhill he could take his regular twelve-mile walks over sarsen-studded slopes and return to that low-ceilinged living-room with its William Morris hanging and Anatolian embroideries, the latter stitched together by Lola who was 'a great mender of things'.

Lola died very unexpectedly of an embolism on the lung in 1963. On those exhausting expeditions which they made, usually in the Easter vacation but sometimes twice a year, to chronicle a new county, she had driven her husband everywhere and their marriage had been exceptionally close. After her death Nikolaus could seldom bear to listen to classical music as it aroused too many memories; and, for a long time after, on visits to Snowhill, he slept out in one of the garden huts, the cottage itself being too full of memories. Fearing that his father might never finish the counties, Dieter drove him around the next carefully prepared and researched itinerary of Hampshire. Thereafter the impetus was restored and drivers were found, but on the dust-jacket of each subsequent volume he described himself first as a 'widower'. Lola had been a Lutheran and Nikolaus had converted to that faith but neither were church-goers – 'vague Deists' is Dieter's description. She was buried in the churchyard of the next parish, Clyffe Pypard, under an aggressively plain headstone with bold 1940s-style lettering by Will Carter, who returned twenty years later to complete the inscription. Now the dark slab reads simply: 'Lola Pevsner born Kurlbaum 1902–1963 and Nikolaus her husband 1902–1983'; though already the grass has hidden his dates.

If this introduction has appeared unduly weighted towards Pevsner rather than Betjeman it is because I have assumed, wrongly perhaps, that the lively profile of John Betjeman's middle years – his teddy bear, Archibald Ormsby-Gore, his enthusiasm for esoteric sects, his television talks on the treasures of suburbia – have made him better known than Nikolaus with his retiring lifestyle and serious pedagoguery. But while Betjeman came over in middle age as everyone's favourite chubby uncle, he was not a particularly prepossessing figure in his youth. He lost his hair early, his wife described his 'green teeth' as his most attractive feature and her friends advised her not to marry that 'horrible little white slug'. Possibly it was to counter this unimpressive physique that he projected an intensely whimsical persona, amusing in that combative public-school manner which reduces everyone by comical nicknames and japes. Pevsner became, inevitably, 'that Prussian pedant' or the 'Herr Professor-Doktor'. His wife Penelope was 'Propeller' or 'Filth' and her legs were referred to as 'Mr and Mrs Broadwood' after the pianos of that name. Yet while I only visited Pevsner's grave for the first time in the summer of 1998 and am unlikely ever to return, I make a pilgrimage every year across the estuary from Padstow and over the dunes to Betjeman's grave in St Enodoc churchyard and always search out inside the church his favourite kneeler, 'the sickly prawn'. His headstone is as dark as Pevsner's, but its lettering is delicately mannered and ornate, surrounded by swirls of Victorian-style foliage.

Here again there are parallels. Both men were deeply involved in the life of London societies, the universities and all the intensely debated architectural issues of planning and rebuilding, so why did they both choose to be buried in their picturesque holiday villages? Is this the flaw, that disastrous Wordsworthian heresy of modern life that rejects the urban for the idyllic rural?

My own association with them both and with that chalk cliff is flimsy, but it exists. Personal associations and prejudices are best aired openly at the start of such a comparative study. As a child I lived in Wantage, under the same escarpment, but a few miles east of Uffington and eighteen from Snowhill. By that time the Betjemans had made their two Berkshire moves and were living next door to me on the other side of the mill-stream at The Mead, a house which John described as 'an ugly little thing in a lovely setting of apple trees'. Mine was an even uglier police house, but it had a garden at the back running down to the clear, fast-flowing stream. Mrs Betjeman took me in the preparation classes for my First Communion but infuriatingly I remember nothing about them except that they always seemed to be held out of doors on the lawn in front of the house. I could only have been seven or eight at the time, born into a Catholic family though now lapsed, whereas she was a convert and died faithful. Since I remember in delightful detail the games I used to play by the stream with a little girl next door and the frightening hissing geese, which the Betjemans kept in their paddock, it does seem hard that I have no clear recollection of my religious instruction by the wife of a famous poet. But I do have vague memories of John himself, already locally celebrated, walking the streets in a long, dilapidated gabardine and a battered hat.

With Pevsner my associations were even less personal but infinitely more profitable. My Oxford doctoral thesis was supervised at St John's College by Sir Howard Colvin who was and remains a very Pevsnerian figure, as orderly and encyclopaedic in his great *Biographical Dictionary of Architects* as Nikolaus was in his even greater, by word count at least, *Buildings of England*, a reputed eight million words. Howard was never overly enthusiastic about the topic of my proposed thesis, 'The Norman Revival in British Architecture'. It was, admittedly, obscure, but it did take in English stylistic perversity over two centuries and I was paternally protective of it. My supervisor insisted upon sound documentary evidence and geographical rigour, the need to include virtually everything built anywhere in England, Wales or Scotland in that deviant native Rundbogenstil, so I would have been absolutely sunk without Pevsner.

Pevsner, predictably, despised and scorned the neo-Norman, but that meant he rarely missed an opportunity to denigrate examples of a contemptible genre so devoid of structural integrity. As for instance in his *Dorset*: 'Plush of 1848 is not archaeologically pure, Melplash of 1845–6 is – worse – Norman'. Things were no better elsewhere. St Mary RC, Manchester, 'shows to what depth of error even good men fall, when they go whoring after strange styles'. St Agatha, Llanymynech, is 'A crazy demonstration of the neo-Norman fashion . . . the windows all shafted, in an elephantine manner'. I could weather the insults: Melplash was a classic neo-Norman jewel, at St Mary's he was only quoting Pugin, St Agatha was Thomas Penson's exotic Angevin, a fantasy expressed in daring polychromatic brick and stone – perhaps it reminded Nikolaus uncomfortably of his own multicoloured terrace house in Hampstead. Though I might disagree with him, there were times when his judgement was sound, and I owe a debt of gratitude to Pevsner for his encyclopaedic coverage.

Let us accept, as we all must, that Pevsner was a scholarly *émigré* who came to this country and drove through, with a selfless yet faintly manic determination, a recording process that the *Victoria County History* series, if it had been organized more realistically, could and should have been completed thirty years before. He made us all look like bumbling amateurs, which is what, in terms of architectural scholarship, we were. Then, because we were so disorganized, because since somewhere around 1820 there had been no national consensus on style, no national policy on the aesthetics of the environment, Pevsner had a clear run to impress his own views on the relevance and superiority of German Bauhaus design – light, simple, stylistic solutions using the resources of modern technology. As the Bauhaus will often feature in later chapters, and as it has been the subject of much subsequent myth-making, an historical note on its origins will be appropriate here.

At the end of the 1914–18 war, depressed socially and economically, Germany had, with its usual drive and determination (those qualities which had got it into trouble in the first place), set out to build enormous new estates, virtually New Towns but not exactly garden cities, of workers' flats. As the Germans were pressed for money these flats had to be both decent and inexpensive. From this successful but necessarily austere building spree Walter Gropius, who had in pre-war days been a pupil of Peter Behrens, the arch pioneer of Modernism, emerged with great credit and prestige. He founded the Bauhaus as an architectural co-operative, socialist and high-minded in its creed, moved it in 1927 to Dessau, set up an architectural school to train the young in Bauhaus ideals and then, in 1928, only nine months later, left to make his fortune in America. The man he appointed as his successor, Hannes Meyer, only lasted two years before he was sacked. Meyer was one of those idealistic Marxists who claim not to belong to any political party. As long as he was in charge, the Bauhaus ideals of strict functionalism and anonymity within the team were preserved. After him, but only for another two years, came Mies van der Rohe, and it was under him that Expressionism and the Cult of Personality began to creep back into the work of the school.

The Nazis closed down the Bauhaus as aesthetically subversive, which it was from the point of view of Hitler's preferred, streamlined neo-Classicism. It was then that the myth of a golden era of self-effacement and social service was born. So when Pevsner was obliged as a Jew to leave his native country and seek his fortune in Britain, he carried with him in his mind this ideal of a simple Bauhaus architecture as a wholesome counter-force to the pomp and blatant Expressionism of Nazi architecture. Mentally Nikolaus was neither Jew nor Lutheran, he was Bauhaus. He was a deeply sincere man and Bauhaus was his creed. It has to be said, however, that this doctrinaire approach was largely a load of impractical, even rather inhuman, nonsense, ill-suited to the modern world and desperately restrictive of the potential of modern architecture in the 1930s.

Against his single-minded determination there should surely have been at least one leading British architect of the old school to put the patriotic counter-case and throw all the prestige of a successful practice, fine buildings recently achieved, a high reputation in government circles, trenchant articles and published works into a war of polemics. Where was Edwin Lutyens? Sir Herbert Baker did fume and grumble impotently on the sidelines, but he was, by that time, something of a relic of imperialism, a heavyweight Edwardian. But where, in a younger generation, were Albert Richardson and H. S. Goodhart-Rendel? The absence of any such architect or even critic ready to theorize and fight back effectively in publications suggests a generation of architects with a death wish.

There was, however, John Betjeman. In the 1930s he was considered a very minor poet, something of a joke even, because his poems rhymed, observed regular scansion and were immediately understandable. Even now at the end of the twentieth century his reputation in some distinguished academic circles is not high, though this is no place to become involved in literary criticism. But some characteristics of Betjeman's poetry are relevant and unarguable. His reputation grew and by the late 1950s he had become a national figure, his poetry wildly popular in a way that only Byron's, Tennyson's and perhaps Kipling's verse could equal. In addition he was a media poet, always ready to make a broadcast or a television programme and to write articles, as often for the tabloids as for the broadsheets.

Unlike most poets Betjeman was more interested in other people than in himself, not in generalized humanity, but in other individuals. When he versified around them it was always within their exact topographical and architectural settings. This is what would, by the 1950s, make him accepted by the media as an authority on style and a champion of the English architectural past against Pevsner's international 'Modern Style'. As early as 1929, in his 'Death in Leamington' – 'From those yellow Italianate arches/Do you hear the plaster drop?' – the precisely named and described architectural setting of the old lady's death is handled with more concern than the old lady herself or her nurse. Betjeman was not only accessible to the average reader, he was specific. Virtually every poem had an exact topographical location in modern Britain, usually in modern suburbia: Harrow, Coulsdon, Woking. The rhyme, the rhythm and the wittily observed architectural detail, affectionately not cynically conveyed, made a wide middle-class readership aware of its surroundings, richly textured by the very recent past. What Kenneth Clark did for European art with his *Civilization* series on television, Betjeman's poetry and media appearances were doing for England's urban, suburban and rural environment. That was a long drawn-out and complex process, with nothing like the concentrated impact of Clark's *Civilization* and its follow-up book. But whereas Clark was preaching to the converted, if indifferent, casual art-lover, Betjeman had to convince most of his readers and viewers, against their existing prejudices, that the despised Victorian stations, churches, suburbs and street furniture were potentially as enjoyable, as visually valuable, as all the previously accepted detritus of our historic past – medieval cathedrals, Georgian houses and the rest. And since, when Betjeman began writing, the nineteenth century accounted for a clear two-thirds of the built environment of the country, this was hugely important. It was like saying 'Beauty of a cranky nature surrounds everyone already. Enjoy it!'

Aside from all the literary debate about the value of obscurity in verse and the importance of an individual poet's religiosity, love life or introspective sorrows, it seems fair to describe Betjeman as the most influential English poet of the century. He was the most objective, the least subjective, the most at ease with himself. Yeats was Irish, Eliot was American, Dylan Thomas was Welsh; but in any case all three were subjective writers, turned in on themselves, each obsessed with sex, drink or religion. Betjeman was as lustful and as fond of wine as the next man, but neither became an obsession, while religiosity could fairly be described as his favourite hobby. The familiar details of the built environment in which we live shape us every bit as potently as our love life, our animals or our drug addictions. Betjeman realized this, hence in 'Pot Pourri from a Surrey Garden', Pam, the 'great big mountainous sports girl', needs the

Surrey backdrop of 'a packet of Weights/Press'd in the sand', 'the Butterfield aisle rich with Gothic enlacement' and the 'remarkable wrought-iron gates' with 'redolent pinewoods' to make her significant. William Butterfield, that least fashionable Victorian church architect, slips through into the reader's awareness along with Pam and her 'arrogant love-lock'.

Paradoxically Pevsner, for all his encyclopaedic toil in recording our architectural endowment, was much less interested in its preservation than Betjeman, less in love with its often messy complexities, far more prepared to take a chance on building a brave new world. On the one side then the English poet, and on the other the *émigré* encyclopaedist.

Their key year was 1930, which was not when an actual confrontation began, but when events started to move towards such an opposition. It was then that Betjeman became an assistant editor of the *Architectural Review*. That was in October. At about the same time Pevsner was in England on his first visit, preparing for a course of lectures which he would deliver on English art at Göttingen University.

Nikolaus Pevsner was born in 1902 in Leipzig, in the kingdom, not of Prussia, but of Saxony. His parents were moderately wealthy non-practising Jews of Russian origin; his mother was an intellectual, his father ran a fur business. There had been an elder brother, but he had been killed fighting for Germany in the First World War. Nikolaus was educated at St Thomas's School, Leipzig, and studied in the usual wandering German fashion at the universities of Munich, Berlin and Frankfurt before receiving his doctorate in the History of Art from Professor Wilhelm Pinder at Leipzig in 1924. He had become a Lutheran and in 1923 had married Lola Kurlbaum, his childhood sweetheart, the daughter of a rich Leipzig lawyer. From 1923 until 1929 he was an Assistant Keeper at the Dresden Art Gallery. Then he became a lecturer in the History of Art and Architecture at the University of Göttingen, specializing in the Mannerist and Baroque painting of Italy. By the time he made his first visit to England he already had a family of three children.

John Betjeman was born in 1906 into much the same merchant middle class, an only child of Highgate parents. His father ran a firm in Islington which manufactured high-class furnishings. The Betjemanns, to use the original spelling, were of German origin not Dutch. John's great-great-grandfather was a Bremen sugar baker who came over to England late in the eighteenth century. After a happy time at the Dragon School, Oxford, and a less happy time at Marlborough, John went up to Magdalen College, Oxford. He never took a degree because he consistently failed the then compulsory examination in Divinity although, as a devout Anglo-Catholic, theology was one of his prime interests, along with the aristocracy, architecture, student journalism and amateur dramatics. There followed two brief, high-spirited spells as a prep-school master, though he had already begun to write seriously and to publish articles in the *Architectural Review* before he joined the editorial staff in 1930. He was still unmarried but had dabbled whimsically in homosexuality and proposed marriage to several well-connected young women, all way above his social station.

So much for their past. Biography is not the prime purpose of this book. It has been written to consider what influence these two men had in shaping architectural opinion in this country from 1930 until the late 1970s when Parkinson's disease removed them both from active roles in polemic, poetry, publishing and committee work.

Opinions on architectural styles change radically within short periods because it is the art form most closely related to human needs and the fickle national psyche. Who would have suggested three decades ago that the Bankside Power Station, erected as recently as the early 1950s amidst a storm of protest, would ever be judged worthy to house a treasury of the nation's modern art? Is it in fact worthy? Does the one deserve the other? Such questions remain open.

Like everyone else I have my stylistic preferences, but as an architectural historian I am particularly aware of the transience of taste. All I can promise is a conscientious effort to present a period of sharply conflicting schools of architectural opinion with as much impartiality as I can summon. I would not have written this book without the stimulus of David Watkin's *Morality and Architecture* (1977), a brave book published at a cowardly time. It posed questions about Pevsner and his influence that have still not been answered, that have been shuffled away by those who find them inconvenient. Architecture has so much capital, monetary and emotional, invested in it that few of us can afford to be entirely truthful. Mistrust me as I mistrust my two protagonists. In the history of architecture there are few absolutes. Nothing will be described as having been for the best or for the worst, nothing will be assumed to have been inevitable, in particular not that march of economic structural minimalism which began with the Bauhaus in the 1920s and which *may* – I insist upon uncertainty – have reached its logical conclusion in the elegant internationalism of Norman Foster's practice. This is not yet another hand-wringing book about 'Whither Britain?' There are already too many of those and no one pays them much attention. The more valuable exercise is to understand how we have been led, guided, deluded and deceived in the past.

CHAPTER ONE

Quaker John in the
Awful Shadow of Shand

No one expects a poet to be absolutely consistent in his views over a whole lifetime. A man as open-minded and as easily influenced by friends as Betjeman went through sea changes; his enthusiasms naturally waxed and waned. In 1932 he was modishly hailing King's Cross Station as 'one of the finest buildings in the world': by 1972 he was dismissing 'grimy stock brick King's Cross' as 'mere engineering'. Someone as given to laughter as Betjeman, with such a keen delight in the outrageous and the absurd, never felt the need to let reality control fantasy. David Watkin recalled him dining in the Travellers' Club one evening when he was indulging in one of his favourite wishdreams – 'What if I had been a schoolboy at Harrow instead of boring, sporty Marlborough?' Betjeman thought Harrow such a deliciously louche sort of school, fast and bad. But then what would have been the most disagreeable college to have gone to after Harrow? Sidney Sussex, Cambridge! 'Harrow and Sidney!' John repeated the dreadful duo, shaking with laughter.

He had a perverse empathy with the unfashionable which gave him a warm sympathy for the premiership of Harold Wilson and the published poetry of Wilson's wife, Mary. Emotionally he was a reactionary, not in any political sense – he remained always more pink than pale blue – but in a cosy, self-indulgent way. If he could find out for himself a peculiar survival of the past, like Sir Edward Maufe's Guildford cathedral, a custom or a person hovering on the edge of extinction, layered with the textures, real or spiritual, of decay, then he was ardently for it. This was what made him, whimsically and mock-seriously, a connoisseur of the music-hall, of indigent Irish peers, narrow-gauge railways and weird offshoots of the Plymouth Brethren.

It is generally assumed that, if a man so armoured with good humour could be said to have had a serious core of religious faith, then the young Betjeman was 'High Church', sky-high in fact. He had served at the altar in Pusey House, Oxford, went on retreats and attended the 1927 Anglo-Catholic Congress on the Holy Eucharist. Anglo-Catholicism had much the same relationship to the main Protestant Church of England that a narrow-gauge system has to main-line railways: lovable variations of operation, complicated rituals that differed from church to church, interesting liveries, double-breasted or buttoned cassocks, 'Sarum' altars with those angel-topped bedposts, and the uniquely insular use of blue in the altar cloths. It was an easy wing of the Church to personalize, with saints as well as the Trinity and with faintly camp Fathers in God; a system to love but also, more importantly, to laugh at when there was a danger of too much rigour or solemnity: the ideal Church for Betjeman.

What is not so often noticed is that his apparent fidelity to the 'spiky' wing of the Church of England was broken for one important and disturbingly inconsistent period of his life. Between 1930 and 1934, when he was trying unconvincingly to persuade his readers that the Modern Movement, straight lines and concrete logic, was the architectural wave of the future, he became a Quaker, possibly in the same spirit as going to Harrow and Sidney, but a Quaker nevertheless. His dalliance with the Society of Friends had begun in 1928. Influenced as usual by an instant friendship with a charismatic person, in this case Gerald Heard, a fashionable mystic who later went on to California and mescalin, John attended a few Quaker meetings and was, in theory at least, converted to simple living. He joined the Society of Friends officially in 1931, something which in his irresolute fashion he had been meaning to do since February 1929, and he only left it in 1937. By that time he may have begun to consider membership inconsistent with his role as a churchwarden of St Mary's, Uffington; though given his flexible sensibility, that is unlikely to have worried him overmuch. There is a 1711 Friends Meeting House in the village, so architecturally the Society would have been more than acceptable. But do the images of Quakerdom and of John Betjeman accord with each other?

The answer must surely be that they do not. He was high-spirited, camped it up convincingly with his homosexual friends, pursued any reasonably attractive woman on sight, loved riotous living and the aristocracy. Some Quakers might identify with such a lifestyle, but not many. His nine-year conversion has, however, to be taken seriously. In so far as the Quakers have an architectural tradition in this country it is one of simplicity: plain walls, tiled roofs and white interiors. But any cult of simplicity in buildings is automatically vulnerable to capitalist economics and cost-cutting. Once simplicity and beauty are seen as nearly synonymous in architectural style, out go decorative detail, aspiration, grandeur and all the engaging pomps and indulgences to which humanity is heir. In their place come sameness, cheapness and urban tedium; and in 1930–5, Betjeman's time as an assistant editor on the *Architectural Review*, that magazine, under the inspired and eccentric editorship of Hubert de Cronin Hastings, was pressing hard for the novel and fashionable simplicities of the Modern Movement as practised with 'clean lines' and concrete panache in Germany, Scandinavia, France and America.

Betjeman had chosen to turn Quaker at a time when the nature of his new employment left him vulnerable to an international style quite alien to his true architectural loyalties. His natural responses were to Gothic abbeys, Regency Islamic domes, Edwardian pubs glittering with cut glass, Victorian seaside dance-halls, shabby Irish Georgian interiors. It is easy, reading the articles he wrote in those years, to find judgements, opinions and subservient eulogies which completely contradict what he would write later, in the years of his fame. But what needs to be remembered is that throughout that time he was suffering from the alien and alienating mental disciplines of an admired and respectable religious cult. A vulnerable and sensitive man, and an easy prey to enthusiasms, he had brain-washed himself into stylistic sympathies which he would later have to disown and attack. In yet another ironic parallel, he had associated himself with an architectural movement which Nikolaus Pevsner had been supporting with conviction, and without any need for a Quaker conversion, ever since 1924.

A case can be made that this Quaker interlude was of no relevance to Betjeman's stylistic pilgrimage, that his Modern Movement heresy was a natural phase of delayed adolescence and that he only later matured into that broad appreciation of all styles, including those of the nineteenth century. But there is evidence against this, quite apart from his informed enjoyment of houses like Sezincote, the Islamic-domed, and Pakenham Hall, the abundantly pinnacled, that predates 1929. On 11 November 1928, before his Quaker winter had set in, he wrote to Ward, Lock & Co, publishers of old-style guide-books to English towns, urging them to scrap their traditional concentration on antiquities of the Middle Ages and appraise in such a town as Leamington 'the statelier late Georgian and early Victorian streets'. 'The sham Gothic of the Parish Church', he wrote, 'is not as bad as your guide makes out.'

For his poetry also, Leamington in 1928 appears to have been a turning-point, a place and a time for empathy with tired old lives and dilapidated gentility. His best-known, most anthologized and already technically perfect poem, 'Death in Leamington', was written in 1928, at the same time as that visit to the spa town which inspired the letter to Ward, Lock & Co. Published in 1929, it was to be far and away the most successful poem in his first collection, *Mount Zion*, of 1932. Indeed it took him several years, after his Quaker phase had moderated, before he was writing poetry again to the same standard; so the Society of Friends may have done as much harm to his poetic range as it did to his stylistic judgement.

What the Quakers cannot be blamed for is the spirit in which John undertook his four terms, starting in April 1929, as a prep-school master at Heddon Court, Middlesex. It is more than probable that this time of spirited irresponsibility was what caused him to delay becoming an official member of the Society until 1931 when the memory of naughty schoolboys with long eyelashes and gang warfare in Heddon Court's grounds had faded away.

In *Young Betjeman*, his admirable and almost too revealing account of John's life up to his marriage in 1933, Bevis Hillier interviewed everyone possible who might have known his subject: the children he taught in his brief prep-school interludes, gym mistresses he flirted with, landladies and cleaning ladies, every kind of friend, platonic and not so platonic, and they all talked with abandon. But the two men who could have told Hillier how they directed Betjeman from his richly prolonged adolescence of the 1920s into the uneasy, stylistically schizoid, poetic journalism of the 1930s were both dead and so unable to supply the revealing anecdotes. Between them John Hope and Hubert de Cronin Hastings put Betjeman, by their commanding friendships, on to the wrong, or, to avoid a pejorative adjective, unsuitable stylistic rails for the next ten years.

It is special pleading to make excuses for Betjeman at this point, but it does seem that he only reached the prime of life in his sixties. He was a very late developer. The converse of this is that in 1929, when he was 23 years old, he was still emotionally a mere boy. If that is accepted it explains his fatuous waste of time at Oxford, his inability to cope with a tutor as distinguished as C. S. Lewis and the childish spite which he was to vent upon Lewis for several years after leaving. As a prep-school master he seems to have been a charming waster, given to gross favouritism with some of the boys and currying favour with them by irresponsible practical jokes, such as lying down in the road pretending to have been run over and then, having stopped a bus, running away laughing when the passengers came hurrying out to his assistance. This was a complicated joke and it must have required considerable nerve to carry it out. Who would knowingly entrust their child to such a dedicated idiot? And yet to be Betjeman, that mocking detachment from ordinary reality could have been a necessary growing stage.

His years at the *Architectural Review* were to be his true university, the time of his late adolescence. It was there, not at Marlborough or at Oxford, that he began to shape what was at that time his deplorable prose style; most of his early articles for the magazine are disjointed and repetitive. He would have to learn to order his facts, brush up on his inadequate history, and eventually, in 1933 on a writing assignment in Leeds, begin to weigh up social and political realities. He was much in need of the two father figures, Hope and Hastings – anything to get him away from the feckless, idle sons of the aristocracy who had been his chosen companions up to this date.

Hope, a card-carrying member of the Communist Party, was the unlikely proprietor and headmaster of Heddon Court where, between April 1929 and June 1930, John had his last uninhibited fling of schoolmastering. As a one-time Shakespearian actor, Hope found in Betjeman a kindred spirit and forgave him his extrovert excesses at the school. Betjeman, impressionable as ever, bought a copy of Marx's *Das Kapital*, not to read of course, and subscribed to the *Daily Worker* for the fun of flourishing it in crowded railway carriages. Hastings was a son of the proprietor of the *Architectural Review* and had, since 1928, been the brilliant and galvanizing editor of that hitherto relatively staid monthly journal.

It is most unlikely that either Hope in his Marxism or Hastings in his crusade for the extremes of European architectural experiment were sincerely committed men. If they had been they would never have gained much influence over the irrepressibly frivolous Betjeman. But a Communist like Hope, who had taught at Eton, kept a butler, relished his Georgian silver and still went at weekends to Hyde Park Corner to harangue the indifferent on the superiority of Soviet Russia, had about him the seductive aura of absurdity, of narrow-gauge steam and clanking couplings. There is a delicious photograph of Hope, or 'Huffy' as he was inevitably called, and John walking together in their full fig of tails to a wedding, both actually wearing, not simply holding, very tall, shiny top hats. John has not gone quite so far as to imitate Hope's white spats and cane, but they both look quite fetching in a rather dated manner. The top hats suit them, they are at home in their antique, though in 1929 still quite correct, clothes. John looks casually distinguished and Hope most formidable. From a man with white spats, an Anglo-Catholic Quaker like Betjeman could easily have absorbed just enough concern for the redistribution of wealth among the downtrodden masses of the proletariat to turn him for a time into a parlour pink, vulnerable therefore to that other kind of revolution, in style not politics, that Hubert de Cronin Hastings was urging.

As for Hastings, while he ranks, if measured by the influence exerted upon a culturally supine nation, alongside Beaverbrook and Northcliffe, he was even more peculiar than Hope. Small, moustached and peppery, he had an uncontrollable aversion to people, hiding away in his office and leaving the meeting of clients and contributors to his Swedish deputy editor, Christian Barman, and dogsbody assistant editors like John. He had only been 25 when he took the magazine over in 1928. By then it had become a ponderous Edwardian relic, heavy with scholarly accounts of medieval brickwork in Aragon or the letters of obscure eighteenth-century architects. A typical monthly issue would open with a genteel water-colour of a church tower in Devon. Then would follow sepia photographs and laudatory descriptions of all that was dreary and acceptable in the narrow range of recent neo-Georgian: banks, hospitals, businessmen's 'seats' in the Home Counties or safe buildings like the Royal Scottish Automobile Club in Glasgow. The journal had a fixation with the ability of modern English craftsmen to equal or excel their predecessors of the 1680–1710 period in keystones, library woodwork and iron railings, while its notion of the 'Modern Movement' in Europe was almost exclusively limited to France. Chichi opulence in marble and veneer by designers like Mme Lucie Renaudot or the Atelier d'Art du Bon Marché featured as very daring efforts. Le Corbusier was sneaked in with 'an apartment which eliminates the unnecessary' but which, with two large oil paintings and an 'Eastern rug', would alarm no one.

Most of the gently dated antiquarianism and detritus of Inigo Jones was swept away within a month of the Hastings take-over. Ruling by a kind of terror at long distance, with sudden telephoned diktats, sensational ideas posted from his holiday retreats, sackings of old troupers, churners-out of predictable articles on nooks and corners of Old London like A. Trystan Edwards, or actual face-to-face interviews with such staff as he could tolerate, Hastings rode the *Archie Rev*, as John called it, roughshod into the twentieth century to become, within a year, a trend-setter that ruthlessly made new reputations and forgot old ones.

Foremost among the contributors whom Hastings brought in to make his magazine a danger to neo-Georgian conservatives and a delight to the lefties of the style world, was Philip Morton Shand, a persuasively bullying journalist in the grand tradition of Ruskinian hyperbole. Shand could make a stylistic theory read like a logical extension to the Sermon on the Mount. Transformed by his prose, chunky blocks of flats in Kensington could rival the Parthenon. His bias and his confidence were a perfect match. In June 1929 he advised readers, 'It would pay to demolish the terra-cotta atrocity known as Harrods *now*, before the loss of custom which will inevitably overtake firms that pin their faith on the efficacy of Victorian glitter compels its directors to do so.' A tall, bald Old Etonian, fluent in French and German and a friend to three of the most celebrated and challenging architects of the European new wave – Walter Gropius,

Le Corbusier and Alvar Aalto — Shand scoured the Continent every year, returning to the *Archie Rev*'s offices in Queen Anne's Gate ablaze with enthusiasm for his latest discoveries in steel and concrete. He was such a lustful man, four times married, that he could literally make the buildings he took up sound sexy. This is Shand selling to *Archie Rev* readers in January 1929 the virility of Easton and Robertson's newly constructed Royal Horticultural Hall:

> Most steel-framed buildings are still-born academic shams, but this naked monolith, with its lean, nervous strength and supple muscular anatomy, lives and exults in living. It is alive because it is of our day, content to live in and express it without the enfeebling aid of conventional mannerisms borrowed from a no longer relevant past.

Even its fittings acquired feminine charm as he enthused over 'that dainty volatile design of the gilded fibrous plaster fanlights in the restaurant which recalls the neo-Baroque traceries and arabesques [no mention now of 'conventional mannerisms' from an irrelevant past] which Oscar Kaufmann has lavished with such a captivating vivacity of invention on half a dozen Berlin theatres'.

Shand had such a natural wordsmith's way with language that he could deceive himself and was often a convert to his own bad judgements. He praised one of his discoveries, a peculiarly graceless German high school in Cuxhaven, because 'The imposts of the main entrance doorway are daringly, but with surprisingly successful results, placed slightly out of axis to the intermediate mullions of the longitudinal window.' Which was Shand-speak for the façade being crooked. As for the obvious criticism, so obvious that Shand raised it against himself — that the school looked like a factory — his glib excuse was that 'light and space are perquisites of both — and indeed their only essentials — and a school is supposed to be a factory of intelligence'. In the whole debate over functionalism in architecture the point that the emotional atmosphere generated by a building is one of its prime functions is rarely aired. For Shand it was enough for a new building to be exciting, and excitement was Hastings's priority in launching features for his new-look magazine.

Lutyens could hardly be excluded from its pages, with New Delhi rising, year by year, like a second Mogul Rome, and Sir Herbert Baker's India House in Aldwych could be given honorary status as 'Modern'. But the fluted-column merchants — titled and double-barrelled architectural practices like Biddulph-Pinchard, Greenaway and Newbury, Darcy Braddell and Humphry Deane, Sir Edwin Cooper and Sir John Burnet and Partners — were relegated to back seats. More wild men took over as regular contributors. In addition to the indispensable Shand there was Frederick Etchells, a genuine Le Corbusier fan, even for a time Evelyn Waugh on the strength of that memorable parody of German modernism in *Decline and Fall* of 1928:

> The problem of architecture is the problem of all art — the elimination of the human element from the consideration of form . . . Man is never happy except when he becomes the channel for the distribution of mechanical forces!

Under Hastings the *Archie Rev* became just such a channel. He chose his assistant editors for their ability to project harsh ideas seductively. Which hardly explains the improbable and in many ways entirely inappropriate appointment of John Betjeman.

In Bevis Hillier's account, John's arrival on the staff came about almost accidentally through the joke- and jape-riddled old boy network. It is far more likely that Betjeman had set his sights on the job. In 1929 the magazine was still acceptably mixed in format, featuring stately homes alongside the ferroconcrete avant-garde, and it paid well; John would begin on £300 a year. There are indications that he schemed, assiduously for someone of his natural playfulness, to achieve an assistant editorship for at least a year before his appointment. The magazine's issue for December 1929 contained Betjeman's pedestrian and hypocritical book review of *The English Tradition of*

Education by Dr Cyril Norwood, headmaster of Harrow. At one early stage the review must have brimmed with what were to become John's standard raptures over Victorian decorative detail, but either it was savagely cut by the editor or John tied himself into aesthetic knots in an effort to catch Hastings's attention by abusing the decorative details that he himself so relished. Whatever the case the review is incoherent, the author's credo bottled up, his preferences denied. Attacking school buildings he wrote:

> How well we remember the writhing gas bracket, the cusped pitch-pine, the terra cotta Queen Anne, the luscious stained-glass window. So well that we fail to notice our own overmantels and the ornamental brick work over our own front doors. That much of our souls is shut.

Betjeman later described the article as 'a monument of dullness', but something about his views must have caught Hastings's errant fancy. Here was a young man interested in that most unfashionable of periods, the recent past, and in the most dated and despised of stylistic detail. With characteristic perversity Hastings prepared to use a second trial piece, with John enthusing about his Victorian obsessions, as a foil to a glitteringly exhibitionist photographic feature on all that was daring and up-to-the-minute in modern English interior design. At the last moment he had an editor's second thoughts or lost his nerve. In his Editorial of the April 1930 issue he took the extraordinary step of quoting something which John had written, but which would not be published until the next monthly issue, explaining that 'what Mr John Betjeman calls the Awf'lly Modern Movement' was a mocking reference to Art Deco, that self-dramatizing 1920s and '30s style of streamlined motifs which Hastings and his magazine rather scorned, and not to the continental Modern Movement, which Hastings revered. As editor though, he still claimed to be 'above party' or above any of the rival styles jostling for public patronage, which he referred to as 'mechanist, Tottenham Court Hotspur, or Mr

Raymond Mortimer's école des Cocottes', meaning Art Deco or Beaux Arts.

In that April issue Hastings was more seriously heralding a major and impressive scheme to bring named artists back into English commercial design, to shake the nation out of its stodgy philistinism and harness fame to merchandising. When John did get his obscure point in about the 'Awf'lly Modern Movement' in the May issue he might have been a little over-whelmed by the dazzlingly photographed project to which his well-intentioned survey of Victorian decorative arts had been conceived as a curtain-raiser.

As Hastings ran it in the early 1930s the *Archie Rev* was an impressive and persuasive journal. The campaign he launched to return artists to a central role in furnishings took the form of a competition to design and decorate a bachelor pad of two rooms, one dining and one living, for a hypothetical peer, Lord Benbow, who was old yet 'with it', a Scot living in London, pro-Mackintosh but anti abstract art. The winning design would be carried out in Waring and Gillow's showroom, which was in itself an attack on the very fortress of wealthy philistinism. The roll-call of distinguished artists and designers whom Hastings had attracted was, for England at that time, definitive:

> Henry Moore, Rex Whistler, Bernard Leach, Clough Williams-Ellis, Paul Nash, Eric Ravilious, Gordon Russell, Gerald Wellesley, Harold Peto, McKnight Kauffer, Vanessa Bell, Duncan Grant, Roger Fry, Serge Chermayeff, Boris Anrep, Basil Ionides, Raymond McGrath, Maxwell Fry . . .

All the great, the good, the innovative and the merely fashion-able were featured and John Betjeman was to be their introduction. It was a remarkable journalistic first but one usually ignored in Betjeman studies in favour of his later *Ghastly Good Taste* of 1933 which only covers the same ground at greater length and in which the writer's Quaker-inspired hesitations between the traditional and the Modern Movement, so apparent in this May 1930 article, have still to be resolved.

Back in the January number of that year Paul Nash had written a peculiarly silly and uninformed article on 'Modern English Furnishing'. This claimed absurdly that 'there has been no established comprehensive style of interior decoration in England since the era of the Brothers Adam, no designer capable of creating a harmony, inside as well as outside of a building, which when completed seemed the expression of an aesthetic'. This omits from British stylistic history Thomas Hope, John Soane, Thomas Hopper, Augustus Pugin, William Morris, M. H. Baillie Scott and Charles Rennie Mackintosh, to name just a few. Even Hastings could not let that generalization pass unchallenged. Besides, he was anxious to remind the nation that in the quite recent past the public had been regular patrons of successful artists. This reminder was for the sake of his competition and his scheme for erecting a 'depot' where English artists and designers could display what they had to offer.

John had been given his orders: remind people of Victorian interiors if you insist, but first you must stress that we are on the verge of a new Modern Movement, a refined simplicity of design that picks up reassuringly where Sir John Soane left off. Second, give the great late Victorian artist-designers like Morris and Mackintosh a good airing: if that involves the Art Nouveau so be it. Then the assistant editor's job will be yours.

These instructions would make sense of a very odd article. John called it '1830–1930 – Still Going Strong – *A Guide to the Recent History of Interior Decoration*'. It is possible that what was 'still going strong' was the tradition of classical simplicity in design, but that point was never made clear. A half-dutiful Betjeman did slip in, before a quotation from Soane urging the contemplation of 'the glorious remains of Antiquity', a very brief and unexplained claim that 'we are only just starting again where Soane left off'. For any further clarification of this point the reader had to plough through another nine pages of John holding forth on his beloved Victoriana before an attack on the Cubists and the 'Jazz' or 'Moderne' style, as Art Deco was at that time variously known, led abruptly into:

The harm they [women practitioners of 'Jazz' ornament] have done is terrific, for now the truly simple efforts of Le Corbusier and Dufy are hardly appreciated. They are merely regarded as 'jazz' gone a little too far. But the work that the French, Germans and Swedes are doing speaks for itself when we bear in mind the axioms of Soane in that their simplicity is the result not of whim but of logic.

There followed another sonorous quote from Soane stating that 'the great beauty of Architectural Composition' lay more 'in apposite decoration than in great Profusion of enrichments'. John must have known perfectly well, if only from the illustrations in his friend Frederick Etchell's 1928 translation of *Vers une architecture*, that Le Corbusier had no time for any decoration at all, apposite or inapposite. But like the rest of the staff on the magazine, converts or fellow-travellers, he had to steer clear of that problem. The very title of the magazine, 'A Magazine of Architecture and Decoration', suggested a commitment to ornament, and it owed a good proportion of its advertising revenue to old-fashioned firms like the Bath Cabinet Makers with their 'panelled rooms in weathered oak', Fenning and Co with their 'Marble Work of Quality', or the Birmingham Guild which claimed to 'have championed the cause of bronze and inlaid vitreous enamel as a decorative medium in Architectural Design', with the chapel at Madresfield Court, Worcestershire, as recent proof.

John's account of general Victorian decoration was confused. Clearly he enjoyed its frills and flounces but with the Hastings eye upon him felt compelled to denigrate it as 'later Regency . . . warped with the German influence', by which he seems to mean 'Baidermeier [sic]'. Blaming the popularity of gas lighting for what he called 'The Peace and Plenty style' of mid-century opulence, he came to William Morris, projecting his work enthusiastically with a poetic appreciation of Kelmscott Manor and the fabrics woven there by May Morris and her Guild. Morrisites he described approvingly as 'proud to sit in a draught beneath a Tudor lattice': this was a pure narrow-gauge comment and a foreshadowing of the true, later Sir John Betjeman of Lost Causes. Ingeniously he suggested that the Art Workers' Guild, Morris's worthy successors, might, because of their empathy with 'an olde worlde cottage in Surrey, earth closets and white-wash', be inclined to 'give a hearing in England to le Corbusier'. This again was John at his most disruptive and mischievous. It would be interesting to know whether Le Corbusier ever heard of his supposed primitive affinity with earth closets.

Unexpectedly John was still faint-hearted in 1930 about the Art Nouveau. Perhaps it held too many memories of his youth and his father's firm. He saw its designs, while 'earnest and natural and pure', as centred overmuch upon heart-shaped water lily roots 'from which a thousand tendrils can drip and tangle'. He found the movement 'aggressively wholesome . . . Every room is made as much like a nursery as possible . . . The windows are opened. Life centres round the bathroom. The whole of England is taking breathing exercises.' But despite 'many a hideous little sideboard, many a sickly front door', the Art Nouveau eventually produced 'one great genius', Charles Rennie Mackintosh. The Willow Tea Rooms and 'A Music Lover's Room' were handsomely illustrated; Mackintosh was described as 'the connecting link between Tudor Revival and Jazz', which was faint praise, but the thought of the proprietress, the famous Miss Cranston, walking between walls of 'old pewter and panels, reminiscent of Beardsley . . . dispensing everything home made − home made cakes off plates made by individual craftsmen' was already vintage Betjeman in his homeliest register of aesthetic strawberry jam.

In 1930, when Betjeman's piece was published, the reputations of Morris and Mackintosh were still at least half in the shade of the unfashionable recently dead, so John was acting as a modest pioneer; 1930 was also the year in which Nikolaus Pevsner was in England getting the feel of a confused and confusing foreign country for the first time and presumably reading that country's leading architectural journal. Did he pick up from Betjeman's rambling article, among all those obscure references to an influx of shoddy goods from Costa Rica, its talk of a 'Jacobean wireless set' and a 'Perpendicular gramophone', a hint that Morris was a pioneer of modern design and a plausible forefather of Le Corbusier, earth closets and all? If he did then Betjeman could have been an influence on the book, *Pioneers of the Modern Movement*, by which in 1936 Pevsner was to stake his first claim to be a British architectural historian, making the flattering suggestion that the Bauhaus and all it stood for were only a natural step on from Morris's version of the Middle Ages.

Betjeman would soon, with his articles on Charles Annesley Voysey, be providing Pevsner with additional material to support this insidious theory. But before that there is the whole world of exciting stylistic distractions in the *Archie Rev*'s gloriously irresponsible pages to consider. Immediately facing John's limp reference to 'the truly simple efforts of Le Corbusier and Dufy', the dashing layout designers had reproduced Marion Dorn's 'Curtain, in Cream and Brown Velvet' for the Combination Room at King's College, Cambridge, a striking abstract design, full page on rough dark paper. On the next page, this time on rough grey paper, was Edward Bawden's wallpaper, 'Cows and Trees', naïvely fresh in pale greens and yellows. These were printed in colour. There followed a torrent of cleverly photographed interiors, half of which supported chaste modernity. The remainder were a deliberate stylistic affront to bold abstraction and direct simplicity, and they demonstrate how far British taste was from the goal to which the extremist members of Hastings's disparate team of contributors were trying to direct it.

Bawden's 'Cows and Trees' was followed by interiors of enchanting aristocratic pomposity, with pilasters of silver leaf sprayed with aquamarine green lacquer and fluted glass, silvered over. There was Oliver Hill's pure Baroque circular garden room at Binfield in Surrey, a seventeenth-century Spanish triumphal door in Clough Williams-Ellis's own house at Hampstead and Gerald Wellesley's neo-Georgian interior panelled 'in Padauk wood' for Sherfield Court, Hampshire. In a more relaxed mood there was a Duncan Grant alcove of mottled paintwork with a meaty plaster nude, and another Duncan Grant fantasy of the bearded Lytton Strachey looking querulously through a frescoed window over a frescoed plant pot and creeper. In 1930 England was in stylistic chaos, looking both backwards and forwards for direction.

That competition which Hastings launched for a design solution to the fictitious Lord Benbow's bachelor pad was won by Raymond McGrath with a predictably austere design of open spaces, geometrical furniture and colour notes of red and green. Paul Nash came an equally predictable second in the same style, but a surprising third was Vanessa Bell with Duncan Grant, in a thoroughly blowzy treatment splodged with colour and soft cabbage shapes. The editor knew he had to hedge his bets.

Ranged against the neo-Georgian, the high camp and the 'Moderne' were Hastings's men, with convincingly simple interiors by Evelyn Wyld and Eyre de Lanux. (Betjeman was always interested in the resonance of people's full names, and some periods do seem to attract their own appropriate nomenclature, none more proper to the 1930s than Hubert de Cronin Hastings.) Easton and Robertson were the stylistic flavours of 1930, their flat in Portman Court – all thick glass table-tops and firm geometry – featured here in the *Archie Rev* and in the rival *Country Life*. The collection of archly lit photographs ended with Serge Chermayeff's own London house, 'the metal work is chromium . . . the dining room's bent metal tube chairs are covered in pigskin', the yellow walls 'give an effect of glowing sunlight'.

The lure of the magazine for Betjeman, and its distorting power over his judgement, lay in this binary appeal. Given his talent for instant friendship with, according to viewpoint, both the style cops and the style robbers, the two-way tensions left him unsure. It was Betjeman's strength not his weakness that he was always vulnerably open to influences. 'Huffy' Hope liked him and more than half converted him to Christian Socialism. Even the remote and peculiar Hastings liked him. So did Shand. So did Etchells. Between them the latter three made him, for a while at least, a functional modernist, though he remained, instinctively and paradoxically, a sentimental traditionalist.

Shand, the gigolo journalist, could appeal to either side. Reviewing Robert Byron's book on the Holy Mountain, *The Station – Athos: Treasures and Men* in 1929, Shand could pen effete, pretentious and largely irrelevant artifice like: 'M. Maurice des Ombiaux, the doyen of French oenophiles has recently pronounced this considered and authoritative judgement: "Parmi les Bourgognes, le Savigny évoque au palais le parfum de la fraise".' Equally he could switch to that vulgar, chauvinistic analysis of the Royal Horticultural Hall. Of course John was impressed and became an instant friend. His social life at this period was unusually fraught as he flitted from one promising ex-débutante to another and he was soon allowing the older man to direct his devious campaign for the hand of Penelope Chetwode and a secret marriage in a register office, leaving her formidable father and mother unaware that their only daughter had made a dreadful *mésalliance*.

Less predictably, and much later, Nikolaus Pevsner was impressed by Shand's views if not by his style. In August 1942, when Pevsner had quietly worked his way into an assistant editor's chair at the *Archie Rev*, he adopted as the basis for his own article, 'Patient Progress – The Work of Frank Pick', a November 1929 article by Shand. 'Underground' was another of Shand's Freudian hymns of praise, this time to Pick, Charles Holden and London Transport. At this period, when the magazine was not losing itself in admiration for Ivor Tengbom's skinny neo-classical Concert House in Stockholm, it was forever enthusing over some aspect of London Transport, its stations or its posters. No one rhapsodized more fervently than Shand, Betjeman's friend and Pevsner's eventual long-range mentor. Shand wrote in his uninhibited Freudian vein:

> It [London Transport] believes and exults in the machine because it has found a new beauty in its functions and lineaments: the beauty of power and efficiency. Like Sex, the machine has come into its own as a result of repression. The Company makes a direct

and unfeigned appeal to the young. It deliberately encourages
them to discard that carefully nurtured inferiority complex: an
exaggerated respect for the achievements of their elders. It seeks
to convince them that they live in a better and more enlightened
age than the last.

Which claim, when cynicism is put aside, was not at the time so
far from the truth. The 1930s would be the decade of Youth
Hostellers as well as the Hitler Youth, and the posters illustrat-
ing Shand's article could take their place in any art gallery. But
is it unfair to add that in his old age the hypocritical Shand
retreated to the depths of rural France to get as far away from
modern buildings as possible?

High-octane journalism in the Morton Shand manner was far
from being Hastings's only innovation for his relaunched magazine. There were colour photographs printed exotically upon
silver paper, captions written like prose poems under dramati-
cally top-lit photography and, at unexpected intervals, moderately witty spoof articles with all the air of John's
irresponsibility but which, by their early dating, June 1930 for
instance, cannot be attributed to him. They were written by
Clough Williams-Ellis, a leading figure in the Council for the
Protection of Rural England (CPRE) and a sworn enemy of all
vulgar commercialism. His June spoof was a double-page
spread of infinitely ugly street scenes entitled 'Oxford (near
Cowley)'. The article promised for 6d. 'Cowley's widely adver-
tised quartier Latin with a guide which shall contribute to the
fuller understanding of her charms'. Beside one exceptionally
dreary street scene was printed 'and creating a newer (and of
course better) world'. Against another was 'Cowley where even
the grocers sell petrol', and under a view of small shops half
hidden by a huge advertisement for 'TYLERS BOOTS', was the
caption: 'A city whose natives have learnt from multiple stores
the art of making themselves understood'.

While he was up at Oxford Betjeman had been obliged to give
up the role of the Fool in *King Lear*, which he had been rehearsing, because of the schoolboy insults he had printed about

fellow-members of the cast in *Cherwell*. These heavily humorous articles in the *Archie Rev* would have been much to his taste. Hastings shared the same sense of humour, only reprimanding John mildly for parading around the office in a very small bathing costume. One article on Greatford Hall, Lincolnshire, in the same issue as the Cowley feature, has all the air of outplaying *Country Life* at its own game with immaculately shot photographs of a grand sixteenth-century country house. But the actual text, by Darcy Bradell (or purporting to be by that successful architect), is not gracious at all but a humorous and irreverent account of how Greatford burned down on the night the author stayed there, with lurid details of his fall down the roof and his rescue of the servant girls. One high spot is an account of the destruction of the eighteenth-century panelling by the flames before, two hours late, the fire brigade arrived.

Another item of humorous photo-journalism inspired by the CPRE, entitled 'Fill up here with . . .', was devoted entirely to a two-page display of twelve petrol stations in various styles: Tudor, Oriental, Georgian, Streamlined and Saucy. It could have been the expectation of similar ventures into architectural wit that initially persuaded Hastings to give John a trial run. He would soon, however, become involved in more serious business and the fledgling journalist would find that, to earn £300 a year, he was expected to develop a flexible aesthetic conscience, and each month to write what he may not have considered to be the absolute truth.

CHAPTER TWO

John the Apostate: Betjeman Wrestling with Stylistic Integrity

With Evelyn Waugh and Osbert Lancaster as his friends and a personal affection for all things complex, crumbling and antique, Betjeman was not ideally cast as the champion of avant-garde Modernism in architecture. By taking on the job of assistant editor of the *Archie Rev* he had put himself in a false position. Ten years earlier someone of his temperament and interests could have mouldered along happily in the same post, writing up dimly symmetrical, hip-roofed, gentry houses of the 1680s and correcting the proofs of contributors on 'Windmills at Bruges', the 'Gardens of Old Spain', or 'Underground Cisterns of Constantinople'. Now, as the 1930s opened up, not only did the *Archie Rev*'s future lie in cantilevered houses on the cliffs of California and new concrete towers by Erich Mendelsohn in Berlin, but it was also caught up in an earnest, though largely ineffectual, debate as nationally revered monuments in England, even the fabric of the City of London itself, came under threat from the developers.

At that point in his life John could reasonably be described as naïve in the best sense of the word – that of natural simplicity in thought – but not as ignorant of what was going on in the world of European architecture. Evelyn Waugh had published *Decline and Fall* in 1928 with its shrewdly prophetic satire on the Bauhaus and German architectural modishness. In the book a Professor Otto Silenus, with a chilling determination to create a true *machine à habiter*, designs a new country house for Margot Beste-Chetwynde at King's Thursday, demolishing a beautiful Tudor building and replacing it with a structure of bottle-glass floors, aluminium balustrades, vulcanite tables and a giant colonnade of black glass columns. Waugh had been alerted to this promising field of anti-German humour by the house 'New Ways' which Professor Peter Behrens of Vienna had designed for W. J. Bassett-Lowke in Northampton in 1925 and which was featured in an *Architectural Review* article in 1926. He had elaborated apocalyptically around that startling suburban invention to create King's Thursday. The fictitious Professor Silenus had designed a chewing-gum factory, the real Professor Behrens had designed a cigarette factory for Linz, Adolf Hitler's home town, a vast multi-layered sandwich of concrete and continuous strip windows. It would be saluted by Shand in the *Archie Rev* as 'probably the most rationally and economically constructed factory of its kind yet built; it is certainly the noblest architecturally'.

In retrospect it was a mistake for John ever to have become, in his warm, trusting way, the friend of people like Morton Shand, Etchells and de Cronin Hastings. They made him compromise his natural judgement and turn his pen to fake apologetics. Yet with them he enjoyed four years of experience, interviewing celebrated architects such as Lutyens and Voysey and working alongside artists and writers like Paul Nash and Robert Byron. He may well have felt, when he formally became a member of the staff in October 1930, that he had to prove himself loyal to this new ethos of the Modern Movement. By *Archie Rev* standards his May article on Victorian decorative art had been entirely heretical. He had even persuaded the design department to illustrate it with a full-page spread of the wildly ornate Edwardian dining-room in Reggori's restaurant in Soho, provocatively captioned: 'Observe the sinister beauty of the hat brackets and the monumental cruet stands. The electro-gasolier

typifies the union of SCIENCE and ART.' To the *Archie Rev* it
typified exactly the opposite. Evelyn Waugh's June contribution
to the magazine on Gaudí, which had maliciously described
Betjeman as 'the chief living authority' on the Art Nouveau,
would not have enhanced John's image.

In an effort to make amends and to toe the party line
Betjeman proclaimed in the December number that easel-
painting was dead. Designers like Paul Nash and E. McKnight
Kauffer, both contributors to the magazine, had, he wrote, realized the true media for artists. These were 'wood and steel and
paper', but also, less predictably, 'mackintosh, linoleum and
glass'. The following February, as a humorous reactionary
counterblast to this revolutionary dogmatism, an anonymous
but most Betjemaine article appeared in the magazine.
Accompanied by a crude drawing, it described a new cottage
'seven storeys in height, the third floor being on top for conve-
nience of access'. In order to eliminate dust it would have no
ceilings and its floors would be composed of steel rods set a foot
apart. With elephantine schoolboy humour it went on to
describe

> walls of glucose and verdigris, painted eau de cologne. To avoid
> unnecessary labour the glass is omitted from the windows, the
> openings being painted in holly-leaf red to exclude all ultra rays,
> while the electric light bulbs are painted black for the same reason.
> The internal doors are of granite coated with Camembert. There
> are no bathrooms but each bedroom leads directly to two cocktail
> bars.

There was to be no repetition of this heavy, Swiftian satire in
the remaining years of Betjeman's tenure. Some topics were
perhaps too sacred to expose to such irreverent wit. The new
assistant editor was beginning to flounder as he looked for a
direction to take in a magazine that was becoming increasingly
alien to someone of his sensibility. In May 1931, obviously after
persuading Hastings to let him loose upon the one subject that
should have allowed him to shine – his favourite country house

– he produced a long, scholarly and completely impersonal account of Sezincote, that enchanted Regency essay in Indian classicism hidden away in a fold of the Cotswolds. It was beautifully illustrated but the text was lifeless and unrevealing of any personality, preferences or experience, which was curious for a man who had spent many happy weekends there with his friends the Dugdales and who should have been able to praise the architecture of the past as movingly as Shand was projecting the architecture of the future.

This failure, for failure it was, raises an intriguing problem in Betjeman's writing. Why should a man who appears superficially to have been such a cheerful and unapologetic collector of like-minded upper-class friends, have written honestly and at length on churches, chapels, towns and transport, but have written so seldom and with such dim reserve on the houses of the aristocracy? In the last half of the twentieth century the English country house has become an icon, almost a Holy Grail, for the middle class, a substitute for religion and patriotism. Every summer season these houses become the objects for Chaucer-style pilgrimages, shrines for the aesthetic refreshment of the soul. Yet Betjeman, that entirely middle-class poet and architectural zealot, virtually ignored them except when mention could not be avoided in a guide. Consider the topics which he evoked skilfully and gathered together in his collected *First and Last Loves* of 1952: Bournemouth, Cheltenham, Aberdeen Granite, Leeds – A City of Contrasts, The Isle of Man, London Railway Stations, Nonconformist Architecture. Where are the stately homes of England? Why did such a populist writer avoid such popular subjects?

There is no easy answer, for he certainly did have a predisposition towards lords and noble ladies. His friend James Lees-Milne made a popular reputation by writing of his experiences with the impoverished aristocracy when working as Historic Buildings adviser to the National Trust during the years of war and the Attlee government. Did John lack suitable invitations or did he have a better developed respect for the privacy of the gentry? He himself could never be described as a private man. Whatever the cause, and a genial decency of nature is the most likely, it saved him from the narrow world which has trapped so many writers on architecture. John had a genuine warmth of feeling for and interest in everyone and, equally telling, in everyone's environment. David Watkin recalls that when he was working on John's papers in the poet's rooms in Cloth Fair, alongside St Bartholomew the Great in the City, they would go out for lunches in pubs and local cafés. And everywhere – one can sense Watkin's bemused delight as he relates it – John became instantly and naturally involved with the waitresses, barmen and café owners, asking after their relatives, enquiring about missing faces, making personal comments to the ladies about their cosmetics, their plans for the evening and the like. This was an instance of that objective feeling for the explicit and the particular which made Betjeman such an unusual and accessible poet, personally classless yet with a keen appreciation for all the subtle markers of the English class system. This could have been what took his mind off the aristocracy long enough for him to become a universal writer. In another instance of the one writer shadowing the other, Pevsner would later display a similar bias towards churches and away from stately homes in the coverage of his *Buildings of England*. But this was partly political, partly to do with his fondness for analysing a building's structural history, and certainly nothing to do with any of Pevsner's interest in what face-powder waitresses might be using.

After this false start on Sezincote and stately homes Betjeman came up with a master-stroke, the only one, in *Archie Rev* terms, in all his four years of working for the magazine. If there was one Victorian-Edwardian architect-designer whose work was simple and functional enough to be acceptable to the *Archie Rev* it was C. F. A. Voysey, and he was still alive, a formidable old gentleman living in bachelor rooms on St James's Street. John persuaded his magazine and the Batsford Gallery jointly to stage a Voysey retrospective and revive the architect's reputation. In the

October 1931 number, two articles were published to coincide with the exhibition. The first, '1874 & After', was by Voysey, introduced generously by Sir Edwin Lutyens, whom Voysey then proceeded to denigrate. Immediately after this came a companion piece by Betjeman, 'Charles Francis Annesley Voysey – The Architect of Individualism'.

Voysey's article was an apologia of sorts, an aggressive and sometimes confusing account of the development of English architecture, not from 1874 but from the Great Exhibition of 1851. It covered the same ground as Betjeman's own 'Still Going Strong' of May 1930 but took a very different line, claiming that the 1851 Exhibition, which John had seen as a showcase for the deplorable 'Peace and Plenty' style, had in fact 'awakened the idea of utility as the basis of Art. All that was necessary for daily life could be, and ought to be, made beautiful.' Voysey's only real complaint about Victorian design was that the new architectural schools pushed the Classical at the expense of the Gothic and also crushed individuality.

All this impressed John enormously. He absorbed without question the preposterous notion that the Exhibition of 1851 had established function as the basis of beautiful design. Throughout his *Archie Rev* years he was to cling desperately to Voysey's central claim that Gothic design had nothing to do with pointed arches or Gothic detail and that it was a system of designing from within outwards, in contrast to the Classical, which was designed from without inwards. In other words the Gothic architect would allow practical requirements of accommodation, plan, aspect and prospect to govern his elevations, while the Classical architect thought first of his façade. Symmetry and balance were tyrannical laws to him.

By repeating the mantra 'Gothic the architecture of necessity', John believed that he could comfortingly describe the most ruthless concrete creations of this new world of Professor Silenuses, into which he had now moved, as 'Gothic'. If the essence of 'Gothic' architecture was practical functionalism, then concrete constructions of the Modern Movement could plausibly be described as the legitimate stylistic descendants of traditional Gothic design. This was to lead him into some para-doxical conclusions: a year later he would be describing the Crystal Palace as Gothic, which was a reasonable conclusion by Voysey's definition, but 'far more Gothic than St Pancras Hotel', which is harder to accept. St Pancras should have been, and indeed much later on would be, a Betjeman favourite, but during his *Archie Rev* years he was very doubtful about it. He had become trapped in a corollary of Voysey's definition: that simplicity was akin to goodness in architectural design, and complexity was less moral. That was a conclusion which agreed neither with the real world nor with John's own instinctive pref-erences.

His uncertainty as a prose writer in these early years shows up in his habit of using long quotations to express what he could not properly express himself and then, at the other end of the quotation, in failing to pick up the thread of the argument. Pugin's habit of wearing sailor's clothes and the long nose which Voysey had inherited from his grandfather, the Duke of Wellington, interested him as much as their principles of build-ing. Like the proverbial dog at a bone, John gnawed away at this theory of Voysey's that 'the individualist is always ready to cast off the shackles of a bygone time and is willing to meet the needs of the present while still holding fast to all enduring qual-ities'. If this excused the revolutionary changes of Professor Behrens then what were these 'enduring qualities' that had to be retained? John was deceiving himself wilfully about Voysey's aims and actuality. A Voysey house – cat-slide roofs, sloping but-tresses, white harled walls, green paint, high windows under eaves – was seductively acceptable to the bourgeois buyer. It was the vernacular past sanitized, a gracious middle-class cottage. According to Voysey several of his earliest clients were Quakers who valued the austerity of his designs and encouraged him to follow this acceptable course of Nonconformist simplicity. Betjeman, now in his Quaker phase, must have found this line reassuring. 'If we cast behind us all preconceived styles our work will still possess a style,' Voysey wrote, and John obediently quoted him. But Voysey never cast away any style, he merely perfected a yeoman's vernacular and brought it up to date.

In all these analyses which Betjeman kept writing for the magazine on the stylistic transitions from Pugin to the present, four in all, he always tripped up on the Art Nouveau. He knew that he must admire Mackintosh, he revered Voysey, yet he could see with his own eyes that both architects were linked to the Art Nouveau movement and that his hero William Morris was working towards it. John's own feelings were, however, distinctly ambivalent. He felt he had to distance Walter Crane and Morris from something unclean: 'nor have they anything in common, as the ignorant suppose, with Beardsley and the twining horrors of the debased *art nouveau*'. His response is puritanical and inconsistent, for at other times he associated the style with extreme cleanliness, limed wood and bathrooms.

In his next and most unhappy contribution to the magazine, 'The Death of Modernism', December 1931, John tried to prove that Modernism was neither dead nor dying but a natural progression from traditional architecture: 'utilitarianism . . . was the child of Science and the Prince Consort', 'traditional architecture . . . draws its vitality from the needs inherent in construction'. In imitation of Shand he referred to 'brilliant young men who create abstract designs' but 'do not ignore the necessary devices of the past'. He pretended to believe that conservatives and modernists were finding 'their way slowly to the middle of the maze, whose magic centre is tradition'. John was becoming a hack journalist, and it got worse:

From the present sightless mass of Greek, Roman, Tudor and Cubist, we are waiting for some monumental architecture to appear that will be fit to house our numberless offices and flats. It is an architecture for artists and not scholars [was he being inexcusably naïve not to anticipate that it would be an architecture for cost-conscious developers?], new materials, a new social order [memories of 'Huffy' on his soap-box at Hyde Park Corner?] . . . a new beauty which this generation must not be too stultified to see.

At least he spared his readers a dawn march towards the rising sun, but it was sad stuff from someone usually so ready to mock any pretentious posturing. Hastings must have thought he needed a rest, but ominously he never let John loose on a modernist building. Instead, in the following month, January, a long and carefully illustrated Betjeman whimsy appeared, an account, treated as if it were a real village, of an ambitious model set up in the grounds of Snowshill Manor, Gloucestershire, called Wolf's Cove. Into its miniature perfections John introduced several of his old homosexual friends from Oxford days as cottage dwellers and millers. For someone who laughed a lot and was obviously great fun to have around, John rarely got his timing right in humorous writing. His strengths were his serious concerns.

In September 1933 he plunged into a pit of gloom with an article entitled 'The Passing of the Village'. This was his very own dark night of the soul. It was probably the experiences behind the writing of this elegy to despair that reminded him of his earlier criticism of Ward Lock's Leamington guide and gave him the idea of writing genuinely inclusive, topographical and architectural guides to the English counties. The first of the *Shell Guides*, his *Cornwall*, would be published in the next year. So he was actually on his way up, but it could not have seemed so at the time. Reading behind the lines of the article, his future wife, Penelope, only daughter of the Commander-in-Chief India, Sir Philip, later Lord Chetwode, was as responsible for its agonized tone as was the Hampshire countryside which appeared to inspire it all. She had insisted on driving around in a dog-cart when that area of north Hampshire downland is best experienced in a very fast sports car with the hood down. Penelope was an animal lover, devoted to horses and goats, her husband-to-be loved people and things. Betjeman was a natural Mr Toad who would have enjoyed a car ride much more. He had once done a ton in his father's Arrol-Johnston.

The gist of the article was that Wield, the small village towards which the dog-cart was jogging, was deserted when they got there. Everyone had gone off to Basingstoke for the day to enjoy the cinema and the chain stores. From several advertisements left flapping around in a porch John imagined with disgust that Hepworths would be making some of them into men of fashion 'for forty-five shillings', others would be chasing 'bargains in underwear', and yet others would be smoking 'Wills Gold Flake' in his pet abomination 'Ye Olde Tudor Restaurante'. None of this would have worried the mature Betjeman – it was all lively human detail and he would even grow to appreciate the charm and pathos of ye fake. But in 1933, together with the dog-cart and Penelope, it was too much.

With a complete inconsequentiality he lashed out in the article at any number of incidental targets. Not only was the countryside finished, but so were Preston, Lancashire, Peacehaven, Sussex, and even Torquay. Preston's 112,989 inhabitants were described as 'persons' because 'one could hardly call them souls'. Peacehaven 'can hardly be called a community. The inhabitants, who have nothing except taste for external ostentation in common, have made every effort to get away from one another'. This from the budding poet of innocent suburban aspiration! Torquay was dismissed contemptuously, with the editorial help of an aerial photograph, as 'looking like a London suburb', which, even from half a mile high, was less than accurate as the coast was plainly visible.

All was lost; of that at least the writer was certain. Soon everywhere would be like 'that blatant mile of pretentiousness, Oxford Street'. Writing sixty years later it is interesting to see how Betjeman got his style villains wrong. 'Commercial Tudor and bank and post office fancy Queen Anne' were his rogues in 1932. By the 1960s he would be hailing them as welcome friends in a desert of blocks with variegated facias. Meanwhile he stressed his conversion to Shand. When the revolution came 'perhaps the house will show its grace of construction in steel and concrete, the petrol station its useful function [picking up an idea from the CPRE about painting the pumps white] and the main road will soar straight and unbothered as a Roman road'.

There was worse to come, much worse. This was one article John would like to have forgotten. Three times he made his point in the closing paragraphs, mentioning 'a civilization which has been brave enough to master the machine', claiming that 'the machine age is in its way a beautiful age' and insisting that 'the Machine has won and England seems to be the last country to realise the fact', and yet his conclusion was entirely sound:

So much misdirected energy is put nowadays into 'preserving the countryside'. Such energy would be far better spent in preserving the towns by disciplining . . . the haphazard planning of self-important local councils.

No doubt remembering that dog-cart ride to Wield he believed that country villages could look after themselves and, as a final bitter thrust of pure 1930s aesthetics, claimed that 'the stateliness of pylons and the clear-cut lines of a new unostentatious factory will not detract from their beauty'. He could not have stooped lower and, as if to emphasize further the triumphant march of Modernism, his article had been preceded in that issue by illustrations of Notre Dame du Raincy, one of Auguste Perret's 1922–3 concrete web churches, and followed by Sir Owen Williams's innovative and glamorously successful factory for Boots the Chemist at Beeston, Nottingham.

There were further trials ahead for a battered Betjeman before his resignation from the *Archie Rev* in January 1935. He delivered a mean-spirited review of a book by Baillie-Scott and Edgar Beresford, defending steel and concrete in the face of their praise for traditional construction. Then came his 'Two Cornish Houses', accounts of Glyn and Boconnoc, which conveyed the Cornish landscape impressionistically but which fumbled Glyn's interiors and everything about Boconnoc, inside and out. In another demonstration of his limited range he wrote for the July 1933 issue 'There and Back – 1851 to 1933: A History of the Renewal of Good Craftsmanship'. As the title suggests this was a rehash of his old material – Morris, Voysey, Gimson – with yet again a confusion of judgement over Art Nouveau. He described it at one point as 'a new and useless structure' but then, a few lines later, changed his mind and decided that 'there was more common sense to it than its wider decorative effects would lead one to believe'. The retreat of the Arts and Crafts movement to the Cotswolds and the failure of its leaders to soil their hands in commerce were regretted. There was, however, hope in the Design and Industry Association, founded by Clough Williams-Ellis, Lethaby, Peach, Heal and Brewer. At this point for the first time there are hints that John was cosying up to Shell Petroleum's publicity people for that invaluable patronage which would support the *Shell Guides* over the years: 'perhaps we stand in the dawn', he wrote. He was right in a personal sense as well, for he had just got married and written his first book.

This was 1933, his year of facing both ways. He became a member for a time of the MARS group, set up by committed architectural extremists of Morton Shand's calibre, to proselytize on behalf of the Modern Movement in England. In addition he published *Ghastly Good Taste*. This is a fascinating little book, perhaps the most revealing Betjeman ever wrote, completely unguarded, an ingenious revelation of the level of his architectural knowledge and of his taste at that time: 26 years old, still a Quaker, still in the grip of Shand and Etchells. If it is read (there were reprints in 1970 and 1986), it becomes clear why Pevsner's opinion of Betjeman's scholarship may have been less than warm. In addition it exposes the critical confusion going on in his mind – a Quaker prejudice in favour of simple solutions, the old Oxford-inspired contempt for the *petit bourgeois*, a natural delight in the ornate and a lack of confidence in the ability of his prose to communicate.

In an Apologia to the 1970 reprint Betjeman claimed to be 'appalled by its sententiousness, arrogance and the sweeping generalisations in which it abounds'. This was fair enough. He also admitted that back in 1933 he had thought Victorian architecture 'was not to be taken seriously, as it was purely imitative and rather vulgar', but then showed that the old arrogance was still alive by adding a sarcastic footnote to his earlier dismissal of the architecture of Richard Norman Shaw.

The actual title of the book is a complete error, one suggested by Frederick Etchells, the Le Corbusier fan, who seems to have dismissed everything pre-Corbusier in that airy manner. Betjeman's whole purpose in writing the book was to demonstrate that there *was* such a thing as good taste in English architecture. It was not 'ghastly' at all; it was the 'Educated Architecture and, Withal, Protestant' of the eighteenth century, the 'reasoned Protestantism . . . of an age not so much of faith as of Sovereign Grace'. This Nonconformist faith was, Betjeman earnestly and persuasively maintained,

> responsible for the simplicity of its architecture. The Quakers, the Baptists, the Independents, the Unitarians, the Presbyterians, whose humble brick meeting-houses, survivals of Commonwealth days, lie hidden away from persecution, deep in the back streets . . . were a chastening influence.

Betjeman gloried in the absence of Rococo architecture in England. 'France was to pay for her *Rococo*,' he gloated: so were 'Italy, Germany, Austria, Spain and the rest of Europe'. The guillotine would exact the price. English classical architecture of the eighteenth century climaxed in the Regency, 'the logical outcome of the Greek revival', an austere perfection infinitely superior to continental excesses of decorative frivolity. Quite soon, within eight years, Betjeman would team up with John Piper, yet another hero-philosopher-guru, and be rhapsodizing about Public House Rococo. But for the moment reserved classicism was the ideal: 'the expression of the serious-minded, reasonable few who controlled it, divided by Theism and Atheism, Antinomianism and Calvinism, and lashed for their faults by Pope and Swift and Churchill'.

That is the core of the book, its earnest message, one reinforced by a vintage evocation of morning service in St John's,

Portsea, the very lowest Low Church Protestantism, a beautiful prose study in blacks and whites: the ceiling white plaster, the incumbent's gown black, the congregation barely visible in the dark woodwork of the box pews. It ends with a serious and un-Betjeman-like defence of the Lord's Day Observance Society:

> Do not despise the English Sunday. When it is gone, like the elegant terrace or the simple brick house in the High Street, it will be missed. Sunday is sacred to Protestantism, and Protestantism purified our architecture.

As a direct result of this pious stance Victorian domestic architecture came in for a terrible drubbing with a clever analysis of how, within a nineteenth-century suburban house, 'a farcical replica of a feudal house is reproduced. Instead of forty rooms, there are four or six.' All the interior detail he later relished was dismissed as 'naïvely snobbish, as unpleasant but as well intended as grocer's port', this last a very Oxford condescension. Even William Morris, after Voysey Betjeman's nineteenth-century favourite, was lacerated by a Shand-indoctrinated Betjeman. He may have come in 'like a healthy breeze, pleading his doctrine of escape', but 'how impossible and how cowardly an escape!' Guild Socialism, 'capable of succeeding only in remote agricultural villages', had temporarily lost its charm for someone torn between Quaker simplicities and the urgencies of a concrete-flexing Modern Movement.

After the war John would nurse a massive inferiority complex about 'antiquaries' with the letters FSA after their names. He believed that they despised him as a non-scholar, a 'wax-fruit merchant', to use his own phrase. If that was the truth his shaky grasp of architectural history evidenced in *Ghastly Good Taste* could explain any number of superior sneers. Somehow, probably by reading too much of Batty Langley's notoriously unreliable 1741–2 *Ancient Architecture*, he had absorbed a mistaken reverence for the Saxons. 'The grace of Saxon architecture and draughtsmanship', he wrote, 'had not been enough for William the Conqueror.' But Norman building ended in 1100 (fifty years

too soon) and then 'the delicate creative genius of the oppressed
Saxons struggled through and expressed itself in Gothic architecture'. Batty Langley lived in a very similar patriotic dream
world, but then, writing in 1741, he had some excuse. Betjeman
in 1933 had none.

The book ends in confused despair. Dutiful to his *Archie Rev*
mentors poor Betjeman declared firmly, 'Steel, concrete, glass
and plywood have made a new era in building.' Then uncertainty set in: 'Only 100 years ago a water closet was unheard of
... There are more swindlers about than ever there were in the
eighteenth century ... Where has English architectural talent
disappeared?' Instead of ending with a firm vote of confidence
in Bauhaus ideals he wrote a last paragraph of pathetic irreso-
lution:

> Architecture can only be made alive again by a new order and
> another Christendom. I repeat I do not know what form that
> Christendom will take, for I am not an economist. It is unlikely that
> it will be capitalism. Whatever it is, this generation will not see it.

Between them, Huffy Hope's Communism, the *Archie Rev*'s
Modern Movement and the Quakers' cult of simplicity had
reduced Betjeman to the stylistic equivalent of a nervous break-
down.

Against these sins of 1933 have to be balanced the virtues of
the poetry published in *Mount Zion* in 1932. 'Westgate-on-Sea',
'Croydon', 'For Nineteenth-Century Burials' and that widely
acknowledged masterpiece, 'Death in Leamington', are anything but condescending or arrogant. Urban poetry is emerging,
relaxed, perceptive and charitable in the best Christian sense
towards the frailty of the human condition and its complex
interaction with urban topography. These are great poems, but
in others, 'The Wykehamist', 'Camberley' and 'The City', a
certain detachment is present. Even 'Hymn', a popular favourite,
with its clever analysis of nineteenth-century restorations of a
village church, only works well if interpreted in the light of the
much later, mature Betjeman who had come round to enjoying

encaustic tiles, marble pulpits and 'Light red and crimson lake' stained glass. As it was first written it was a condescending joke from someone who had still not come to terms with the attraction which the Victorians had obviously always exerted over him. But the rhyming scansion and the timing were already irresistible – he had found his poetic voice but not always his aesthetic judgement.

There was a parallel weakness in human reach when it came to those Modernist houses that were beginning to appear in the better-class suburbs and in choice rural settings. Why did John not write them up sensitively for Hastings? Seen from a very late twentieth-century perspective they have an enormous individuality and charm. Why was John waiting always for this new architecture to emerge? 'Whatever it is, this generation will not see it' was the last line of *Ghastly Good Taste*, and he had concluded that book review heaping ordure on Baillie-Scott by complaining about 'the age in which I am unlucky enough to live'.

These angular concrete houses were the new age. It had already arrived. Today we join groups like the Twentieth Century Society and travel around enjoying and inspecting their daring variety much as we do stately homes or Early English parish churches. They are the challenging folly towers of their time, ornaments to every landscape fortunate enough to boast one of them. They should have fallen straight into Betjeman's narrow-gauge category like 'The Sandemanian Meeting-House in Highbury Quadrant' or Aldersgate Station, characterful, lovable rarities. Alan Powers has written in the Twentieth Century Society's journal a perceptive analysis of how, in their first years, they were surrealist gestures, impossibly pure living units, the Platonic idea of a 'house', that could never be photographed with an untidy human being sitting in a severe chair or dirtying the pure area of a vacant wall. To build one and then live in it was a surreal adventure, a waking dream state. The marble Rococo chimneypiece that Denys Lasdun put into the minimalist purity of 32 Newton Road, London, in 1938 was a considered poetic emblem of the alienating absurd.

Pen Pits, Penselwood, was the kind of 'narrow-gauge' house that Betjeman could have delighted in. Built in 1935 for the composer Sir Arthur Bliss and his American wife, Trudy, it is entirely surreal in its deliberate defiance of the orchard land-scape in which it sits near Stourhead Park. There was never any intention that it should fit in. Instead it fights against its rural setting with its insistent horizontals and vast sun-deck above a porch almost as extravagant. On that bare roofline above the huge picture windows a chimney outlined in blue and a water tank jut up like ship's funnels, as if the whole absurdity could sail away into the woods. Peter Harland designed it deliberately as a sham. It is built of brick but its walls are rendered to make it look as if it is trendy Modernist concrete. There is a wonder-ful stagey photograph of Harland and Bliss poised in ridiculous attitudes with Harland half-way up the ladder to the sun-deck. Both men wear the country uniform of the period – plus-fours and pipes. The house is fun, a game, a play, and they are the actors. It was even lit by oil lamps and because there was no electricity Bliss had to use a wind-up gramophone: in no real sense was it modern, so it should have appealed to John. Bliss played ping-pong, a very Thirties game, with Ben Nicholson, Trudy Bliss made rugs to Nicholson's designs, Paul Nash stayed there and painted the Pits, a prehistoric earthwork. It was the epitome of its decade, a house for Osbert Lancaster to draw but not one that Betjeman would have relished; he seems never to have found fake concrete as comical as fake timbering.

In September 1933 Betjeman was deeply involved, not with any metaphorical narrow gauge, but with real railways. 'Dictating to the Railways' in the September issue and 'Leeds – A City of Contrasts' in the October number were to be his last two contributions of any substance. The first was an ill-aimed grumble, the second a small masterpiece of urban response, a marker to the way ahead, to the true 'people's John'. After Leeds he was ready to fly, to go freelance and to be an opinion-shaper, a righteous journalist.

Even so, almost everything about 'Dictating to the Railways' was ill-judged. For a start he wanted to demolish Victoria and Waterloo to build a giant terminus at the Elephant and Castle. Then, still obsessed with dreary simplicities, he insisted that the railway sheds of the old GWR broad gauge were 'as much a part of the landscape as barns and farmhouses . . . so [thus] one day we will see pylons'. Then, in an illogical leap, he insisted that Waterloo, Marylebone and St Pancras would never fit easily into any landscape. King's Cross, however, would with its simple roofline, and so, at a pinch, might Euston. It was with Euston that he made misjudgements which were to count against him in future years where the Victorian Society, a powerful statutory body, was concerned. When they came to appoint a new Chairman it would be German Nikolaus whom they chose, not English John even though he had been a prime mover in the Society's foundation. He only allowed Euston provisionally on to his honours list of simplicity. 'For many years now', he noted, with no sign of anger or protest, 'there have been rumours about the demolition of its Great Arch.' He was referring to Philip Hardwick's noble Doric triumphal entrance which was eventually demolished to nation-wide dismay in 1962. Back in 1933 John was airily unconcerned with such relics. What was needed was a clean sweep of Euston's clutter, organized by 'a proper architect'. If as a result 'the Great Hall [by Hardwick junior] must go, then that is that; and if the arch must be demolished, then that is that too'. It would be interesting to know if he remembered that cruel judgement when he wrote a delightful poem in 1973 to protest against the 'Sack of Bath':

> Goodbye to old Bath. We who loved you are sorry
> They've carted you off by developer's lorry.

Times change and we change with them. For his last pane-gyric on Leeds all Betjeman's previous sins and lost opportunities on the *Archie Rev* should be forgiven. It may have begun with a despairing sigh from Hastings when he saw on his desk the photograph of E. Vincent Harris's newly completed 1933 Civic Hall at Leeds. Here was a building so dreadful, so aggressively neo-Georgian by the canons of the *Archie Rev* that only Betjeman could be sent up north to cover its official opening. He went on a railway journey, past disused branch lines, smoke-blackened farms, mills and factories 'TO LET', into the heart of the Depression, to a city where 'the rain seems always to be falling'. And it was in Leeds that Betjeman, the precious young Londoner, until then a dilettante of architectural finesse, underwent his conversion. To understand Leeds, he wrote, 'one must acquire a Leeds sense of proportion. And this is done by realising two things about Leeds. First it is a Victorian city. Secondly it is parochial. These two qualities are far more blessed than is generally supposed.'

Throughout his previous three years at the *Archie Rev* John had been struggling against his natural attraction to things Victorian, trying to rationalize it away as philistine and unworthy. But now, among Alfred Drury's naughty lamp standards in the City Square, 'nudes representing *Night* and *Morning*', mills and warehouses that were 'the cathedrals of the industrial north' and the 'black Protestant northern Gothic of the Nonconformist conscience', he became an L. S. Lowry among poets, but with a much broader range of appreciation than Lowry ever commanded. He walked the streets of back-to-back houses where even 'the saddest, dingiest little lanes' were decorated in red, white and blue favours. 'Everyone had gone to see the King and Queen. Suddenly bells peeled out under the clouds and even louder than the bells came the cheering . . . the sun came out and down the steps of the Town Hall came the Queen in white . . . The city was alight with excitement.'

And so was he. Betjeman had discovered populism and was beginning to see that buildings had as necessary a role as events in ordinary, provincial lives: the charm of the bungled, the second-rate and the amusingly memorable. Chatting to Yorkshire folk in their pubs and in 'a comfortable semi-detached residence in the Tudor style' (never a description he would have allowed himself in his earlier persona) he learned that for them Harris's creation was 'the most beautiful Civic Hall in the world'. And so he too discovered its beauties. In reality the building was not so much neo-Georgian as Wren suffering from double vision; but in those honeyed tones of critical charity that were to become nationally famous on radio and television, he declared 'Photographs have not done the building justice.' The twin steeples, versions of Wren's St Vedast, Foster Lane, were not, he decided, meant to be seen together, even though Harris had set them one on each side of a massive four-columned portico. Instead the passer-by 'suddenly catches a glimpse of one or other brilliant white steeple rising above tram-lines and turrets, terminating an otherwise dreary street'. It was the kindest of perceptions and it was to be his way ahead. He would go on, still with a scholarly eye for dates and architects, but enjoying provincialism wherever he travelled, in small West Country towns, in seaside dance-halls, in desolate Lincolnshire churches and, above all, in suburbia where ninety per cent of his readers lived. Betjeman would teach the English to see and to appreciate the poetry of the ordinary, and it all began in Leeds in 1933.

CHAPTER THREE

How to Catch a Pixie: Shaping the Great *Shell Guides* of the 1930s

The year 1933 was a restless and uneasy time for Betjeman with that Leeds article a rare sign of deepening perceptions. He and Penelope Chetwode celebrated their wedding in furtive secrecy on 29 July after a courtship which had been anything but confident and smooth. By all conventional lights she was marrying beneath her; John's Irish friend Lord Clonmore had actually advised her to drop him before it was too late. If you are in pursuit of the only daughter of a baronet and the C-in-C of the Indian Army, then a salary of £300 a year for acting as a general dogsbody on an architectural magazine begins to seem inadequate, so John was casting about desperately for ways to get richer. He had made a friend of 'Beddi-ole-man', Jack Beddington, the Director of Publicity for Shell, who was eager not only to encourage drivers to use more petrol but also to associate his company with a caring attitude to the environment. Between them the two men persuaded the *Architectural Review*'s controlling director, Maurice Regan, that with subsidies and guarantees from Shell, a series of county guides would be a profitable venture. Betjeman was to be their general editor and his salary would be raised to £400 a year to cover this extra work. In order to encourage the interested parties he had produced early in the year a 'dummy' guide to his favourite county, Cornwall.

On the strength of that rise he had married, but after a few days honeymooning in an Essex pub, Penelope went back to live with her parents and wait for an auspicious moment to break the news to them. During these disturbed months, more concerned with an elusive Penelope and financial problems than with subtleties of style and mood, John had been writing *Ghastly Good Taste* as well as that dummy *Cornwall*. Then to his fury he was told by Maurice Regan that, while future authors would be paid £50 for writing each *Shell Guide*, the £50 for his *Cornwall* would have to come out of his £100 salary increase.

That was probably the gesture of mean caution that decided his eventual resignation. In the meantime he was forever exploring the possibilities of going freelance, though in his Walter Mitty moments he claimed that he was already the acting editor of the *Archie Rev* and would be editor in name also within a year.

Betjeman's eventual reputation as a poet makes it hard to grasp that at this stage in his career his skills were technical and artistic rather than literary. In a letter applying for a post with the publishers Hamish Hamilton, he stated that 'make-up', the process of laying out print and illustrations to make up a page, was 'always my chief delight'. He also rated himself as a photographer. On the other hand in three years at the *Archie Rev* he had not produced a single feature that could be said to have advanced the journal's position at the cutting edge of modern architectural polemics, nor had his recycling of nine-teenth-century art history been confident or even positive. But when he claimed, in a letter to Jack Beddington of 17 August 1933, that the prospective *Shell Guides* would be a failure if Maurice Beck handled 'the aesthetic side of it', he was being absolutely sincere. The quality and colour of the paper and the endless varieties of type fascinated him. It was the look and feel of a book, not its prose style or its message, that were his primary interest and he believed that only he could launch the series effectively. He tried desperately to persuade Beddington to write into the contract that, as well as making him general editor, all matters to do with make-up, illustrations and letter press should be in the hands of 'Mr J. Betjeman'.

Personally I find the layout of the title page of John's first Shell venture, *Cornwall*, a mannered, confused and thoroughly off-putting tangle of ill-assorted typefaces, and much of his prose in the subsequent pages is as formal as that in *Ghastly Good Taste*, which must have been written at almost the same time. There is, however, a curious paradox at work here in values and influence. Betjeman's poems − compact, memorable and anthology-friendly − will inevitably outlive his guidebooks which, by their nature, were bound to date. But in their first twenty years, from the publication of *Cornwall* in 1934, it was the *Guides*, not the poetry, that were the more influential. Thirteen had been published before war broke out in 1939 and each, at two shillings and sixpence a time, was an innovative prodigy of photography, layout and reassessment.*

The *Guides'* peculiar good fortune was that for the next twelve years, through the war and the Labour government of 1945−51, they would have a captive audience and very little competition. For throughout that period the country was in austerity, thrown back on its own resources. Paper was rationed and libraries made do with the stocks they had accumulated in the previous decade. In many ways it was a last chance for England to be insular and English; a time for cyclists and walkers, with petrol severely rationed and foreign travel at first impossible and then limited by meagre foreign exchange allowances. One result was that an entire generation of the intelligent middle class and aspirant lower learnt to explore their counties from

---

* *Cornwall* − John Betjeman (1934); *Wiltshire* − Robert Byron (1935); *Derbyshire* − Christopher Hobhouse (1935); *Kent* − Lord Clonmore (1935), *Devon* − John Betjeman (1936); *Dorset* − Paul Nash (1936); *Somerset* − C. H. B. & Peter Quennell (1936); *Buckinghamshire* − John Nash (1937); *Hampshire* − John Rayner (1937); *Northumberland and Durham* − Thomas Sharp (1937); *Oxon* − John Piper (1938); *The West Coast of Scotland* − Stephen Bone (1938); and *Gloucestershire* − Anthony West (1939).

Shell Guides. These were bound on spirals like school exercise books yet they exhibited all the enticing, flashy tricks of presentation that the *Architectural Review* had pioneered in the glory days of Hubert de Cronin Hastings. Every public library stocked them and no other contemporary guide – Kelly's, Murray's or those of Edward Burroughs – came near them in design or in the shocking honesty of their writing. They brimmed over with an intelligent irreverence for established judgements and dry antiquarian appraisals. Their sensitive appreciation of the less obvious made dim counties like Buckinghamshire, Derbyshire and Durham seem as exotic and characterful, as crammed with potential discoveries, as the conventional holiday lands of Cornwall, Devon and Dorset. When Betjeman wrote primly in the Preface to his *Cornwall* that he was drawing attention 'to the many buildings of the eighteenth and nineteenth centuries that have architectural merit', it is unlikely that he realized quite what a genie of revived aesthetic evaluation he was about to release. To read a *Guide*, or even to turn the pages of one, skimming its captions and marvelling at its photography, was to become an informed convert to architecture and an aficionado of the environment.

The *Shell Guides* taught, though this is a sensitive subject, a practical patriotism. After reading them and using them you thought, and you may have been right, that you knew what you loved – an historic and accessible countryside, dense with the textures of the past. That was one impact. On a subjective, personal level it was while editing them that Betjeman at last found his ideal and distinctive voice, one to which he had been moving uncertainly in the *Archie Rev* and missed entirely in *Ghastly Good Taste*. Between the first, *Cornwall*, and the fifth, *Devon*, two years later, there was a huge leap in subtlety. When John Piper came in 1938 to write the eleventh *Guide* on Oxfordshire, he thanked Betjeman for making everything possible 'by writing what I regard as the model *Shell Guide* for all time, Devon'. And if, on a ruthlessly honest assessment, Piper's *Oxon* was to prove marginally superior to its model in photography and sharpness of comment, then John still deserves the credit for casting the mould.

His poetry worked fascinatingly alongside the *Guides* and his first broadcasts on places and buildings for the BBC. *Mount Zion* of 1932 had in itself been a topographical experiment. In those brash, exciting 1930s Betjeman was sufficiently self-confident to enjoy being influenced and impressionable. Edward James, the millionaire eccentric and art patron who paid for *Mount Zion* to be published, pressed him into a little quirky surrealism of presentation, 'this precious hyper-sophisticated book on green paper', as John described it in the Preface. Even more important was Hastings who illustrated a number of the poems – 'Croydon', 'Camberley', 'The Outer Suburbs' – with his notably untalented sketches of suburban housing. Hastings, who once gave a lecture with his back to the audience and who shunned any personal contact with contributors to his magazine, was naturally drawn to the suburbs by their anonymity as much as by their variety. It was he who first sold suburbia to Betjeman, whose instinct had been to despise it; and it was suburbia which would make John the laureate of the middle class of southern England. In 1940, by which time the flow of the *Guides* had been cut off, *Old Lights for New Chancels* was published and that contains 'Bristol and Clifton', the very essence, not of suburbia, for Betjeman rarely generalized, but of a particular suburb; and that poem put him right up with the very best of Browning, surpassing even Browning's 'My Last Duchess', for Betjeman had no need to take refuge in Renaissance Italy to deliver his insights into the human condition. Humanity had spoken to him on Clifton Green, not Rome of the Cinquecento. In this one poem he captured with deadly precision the tensions within the Church of England and their physical manifestations within a church interior. Read it if you have missed it and you will never take differences in ecclesiastical ritual too seriously again.

Yet in 1933 he was still listening only to the smart, cynical chatter of his upper-class friends and his Bauhaus-obsessed colleagues on the magazine. As a result the tone of both *Ghastly Good Taste* and the *Cornwall* dummy was one of arrogant didacticism, the prep-school master telling a readership of semi-ignorant small boys what to think, even though, at that moment, he was far from sure what to think himself, other than that the Regency had been a time of elegant refinement. This was hardly a perception worth voicing, but it was a standard fall-back point in Morton Shand's arguments.

Cornwall, which was only that dummy revised and improved, has few of the virtues of *Mount Zion*. Launceston Castle for instance: 'for those who are interested in ruins, it is a ruin'; Callington: 'the unimportance of the place will commend it to those who need a rest'. Even Pevsner, coming to the same subjects seventeen years later in his 1951 slim, paperback *Cornwall*, wrote with more visual perception and human feeling. His Callington read: 'The little town, not specially attractive, is dominated by the great chimney of a disused mine on Kit Hill, looking from the distance like one more Wellington Testimonial.' When he came to Launceston Castle he not only gave a history of its foundation and gradual ruination, but also noted of the North Gate: 'When Howard visited it in 1779 it had no chimney, no water, no sewers, and damp floors. The prisoners were chained together.'

Comparing the two *Cornwalls* underlines the need to avoid stereotypes of the two men. Betjeman could at times be as schoolmasterly as Pevsner ever was. Picnickers were warned not to leave litter, told that oil of citron and lavender would keep away the flies, but that 'if you only try to like wasps they will like you'. The younger Betjeman had two hobbyhorses, typography and third-rate nineteenth-century descriptive poetry and prose. He rode both horses hard in *Cornwall*. Most of his gazetteer account of Boscastle was taken up with a stilted description of the place from an early guide by Redding. This claimed that 'no spot in the world could be more calculated for philosophical retreat' and described 'a silent tower from whence the merry peel has never been heard to break upon mortal ear'.

A philosophical retreat by a silent tower was no sort of offering for the average guide-buying twentieth-century holiday-maker, however refined in sensibility. Even Redding's desperately dated humour was passed down to convey Betjeman's distaste for a modern holiday resort like Bude. A visitor to the town addresses a waiter:

> 'A little water. There is none in the teapot.'
> 'Yes, Sir.'
> 'Can't you bring in a tea kettle?'
> 'The urn is coming, Sir; we don't use kettles like the Stratton people!'

That might have been enough to set John's aristocratic Irish friends rocking with genteel laughter, but in a guide intended for the bright young things of the Thirties it was as dead and incomprehensible as the caption to a nineteenth-century *Punch* cartoon.

This prevailing tone of foolish contempt for 'enjoyment of a distinctly popular nature' was worlds away from his appreciation of Leeds or the later, wiser, middle-aged John's pleasure in the spectacle of a thousand couples 'moving beautifully' in the Palace Ballroom of Douglas on the Isle of Man. Indeed the entire balance of information in his *Cornwall* was ill-judged, far too close to a conventional Kelly guide to seem relevant and fresh. That eye-catching blast of discordant typefaces on the title page promised, in the style of J. P. Neale's *Seats* of the 1820s, 'Castles, Seats of the Nobility, Mines, Picturesque Scenery'. Then in separate compartments came the information which should have been brought together in a comprehensive gazetteer: Ferry Services, Towns (but no villages), Prehistoric Cornwall, The Age of Saints, Churches (several pages away from the towns which they served), Golf, Hunting (as if Cornwall were a popular hunting county or as if more than one visitor in a thousand would wish to attend a meet), Tide Table, Fishing, Sailing, Bird and Plant Life, Plants, Birds (*sic*), the Cornish Language, Cornish Food, Isles of Scilly, Picnics.

As a result of this subdivision the gazetteer, if 'Towns' can be so described, was only a few pages long and the entries miserably grudging on facts and devoid of atmosphere. Lostwithiel for instance was covered by 'The bridge at Lostwithiel, which is a mediaeval building, is well worthy of note. The rest of the town has nothing of architectural interest beyond its church to commend it.' And when the reader turned through the pages to find Lostwithiel church in a section laid out like a railway time-table, there was only staccato jargon: 'Church. 13th and 15th cent. tower and spire: clerestory: late Decorated tracery in E. window: 14th cent. font: 17th cent. alms dish. over restored 1882.' Betjeman was offering no trace of affection or of feeling for stonework, colour or individual character, merely the kind of antiquarian notes that had been doled out in standard guides for the last hundred years. Even more dismaying is the discovery that, though John had by then been an enthusiastic church crawler for at least eight years, he had still not developed a feeling for communicating that interest. Lostwithiel in his rewritten *Cornwall Shell Guide* of 1964 would become 'an old town full of character and hidden beauty', and be written up by an appreciative John in two printed columns of more than 800 words. An eighteenth-century granite grammar school, a medieval Duchy Palace, several Methodist chapels and a 1740 Guildhall would all feature, as would an account of the town's role in the tin mining industry and its navigation on the Fowey. Where, in 1934, had Restormel House – 'Strawberry Hill Georgian Gothic' – and G. E. Street's 'picturesque little verger's house' in the churchyard been hiding?

In 1964 an entirely different Betjeman was writing. 'High' Victorian multi-coloured brick and stone banks were no longer described with that all-purpose adjective 'hideous'. Truro Cathedral in 1934 had been 'in the E E style, not suited to Cornwall . . . an interesting essay in the Victorian manner and the correct Gothic style'. By 1964 'this cathedral is the first and to me the most interesting cathedral built since St Paul's in England'. That was followed by an enthusiastic 400-word

analysis of Pearson's intentions and successes. The church of St
Protus and St Hyacinth at Blisland was accorded in 1934 the
brief '15th cent. tower and nave: restored in 1896'. In the later
Shell Guide it has a smokily textured, full-page photograph and
a lovingly evocative description of its 'dazzling and amazing'
interior:

> Granite columns, leaning this way and that, support barrel roofs
> with richly carved ribs and bosses between their white plaster
> panels. Across the whole length of the church is a wooden screen
> highly coloured with loft and rood above it and glimpses through
> to twinkling altars.

Those church lists of 1934 could so easily have been enlivened
if, instead of corralling 'The Age of the Saints' in a separate
section with mocking drawings by Hastings, he had attached
their individual legends to their particular dedications. How
much richer those drab lists of salient features would have been
if they had been linked with St Petroc obliging a woman to
regurgitate a three-foot salamander after she had inadvertently
swallowed a newt, or St Crantock and St Ternoc losing their
claims to holiness – Crantoc's leprosy and Ternoc's seven iron
belts – after taking hot baths.

The 1934 book concluded with what was to become in future
Guides, Shell's ritual commercial play on place names:

> Landeglos by Fowey but Motorists buy Shell
> You can be sure of Shell.

Even so Shell's publicity department could hardly have felt very
sure of John Betjeman after that first, far from populist, performance. His touch was anything but light. That inexplicable
enthusiasm for the worst kind of Victorian travelogue was still
handicapping him and it is obvious why his good friend Piper
tactfully praised *Devon* and forgot *Cornwall*.

The major structural flaw in *Cornwall* was put to rights in the
three *Shell Guides* which would appear in 1935 and which were
with the printers even as Betjeman was writing his *Devon*.

Wiltshire by Robert Byron, *Derbyshire* by Christopher Hobhouse, and *Kent* by Lord Clonmore each had an extensive gazetteer where villages as well as towns were listed and where churches were included with all the other buildings. That would now be standard practice for all the *Shell Guides* except the brilliantly idiosyncratic *Hampshire* of 1937 by John Rayner. But simply moving to an alphabetical gazetteer cannot explain the shift in tone and mood that is so evident in *Devon*. In marked contrast to *Cornwall*, *Devon* was seductive and, in places, positively elfish. Scattered at random in nooks and crannies of the gazetteer and its attendant essays were whimsicalities which John had culled, not first-hand from old gaffers over pints of cider in roadside ale-houses, but from 'Librarians of London University Library (Folklore Section)'. So readers were warned in a special italic type, and in all apparent seriousness:

> *Whitchurch Down is very dangerous from pixies. They lead you a dance so that you lose your way, especially if you are old and feeble. If you turn your pockets inside out you will be safe. Another precaution against pixies is to take off your coat, turn it inside out and put it on again!*

As another psychic precaution:

> *If you see one Magpie, which means bad luck, spit over your right shoulder three times and say:*
> > *Clean birds by seven*
> > *Unclean by twos;*
> > *The dove in heaven*
> > *Is the one I choose.*

While an adder, if you were unlucky enough to meet one, could be charmed into harmlessness:

> *Draw a circle with an ash rod round it and it will not be able to move from the circle. Then light a fire in the circle and the adder will go into it. If you are bitten by an adder* [a likely eventuality if this rigmarole was ever performed] *you may be cured by having a collar woven of ash twigs hung around your neck.*

Perhaps the most delightfully perverse of Betjeman's devices to avoid the tedium and predictability of *Cornwall* was his entry for Exeter, the county town. The first, and at that time staggering, indication of the *Guide*'s individuality was John's dismissal of the cathedral as disappointing, with the shrewd perception that its west end was 'singularly ill proportioned'. This was not, in the 1930s, the kind of thing one said about a major ancient cathedral, but there was a stimulating measure of truth in the observation and it created a healthy critical spirit in anyone prepared to weigh it up thoughtfully. Henceforward how would one judge stocky Rochester or plum-pudding coloured Chester? That was the true shock value of a *Shell Guide*. But the provocative John was not finished. The city's importance lay in the fact that 'today farm labourers come to consult the great white witch of Exeter, the greatest white witch of the West, if their horses are ill or their cattle have been "overlooked"'. The witch was a man, and John solemnly assured his readers that he wore a white metal button and his cures were 'most effective'.

Devonshire superstition was only the liberally applied icing on the cake, John's pure, unscrupulous journalese. The *Guide* was also, as with that west front of the cathedral, educative and challenging. Betjeman was right to take his make-up, his aesthetic handling of the *Guide*, seriously. One photograph of Barnsfield Crescent in the city was bled right across the page into a compelling pattern of insistent fenestration with not a scrap of relief from sky or foreground. Faced with that the reader could not avoid thinking about windows in façades and how their geometry worked to make or break a building. Then, as a follow-up, to test how the lesson had been absorbed, John featured a smaller photograph of a starkly elegant lace factory in Tiverton, eighteenth-century and six storeys high, entirely plain but built on a slight curve, 'storey upon storey of well proportioned windows in subtle gradation'. If the reader, force fed on the aesthetics of Barnsfield Crescent, could take that austere lace factory then the lesson of appreciation had been consolidated. In future there would be no going back to blind indifference. The lessons of snazzy presentation picked up in the offices of the *Archie Rev* from Hastings were being employed to turn every intelligent tourist into an aesthetic critic, environmentally aware, able to notice beauty in unexpected places, to downgrade a cathedral and upgrade a factory.

Sometimes, reading *Devon*, it is difficult to believe that a hard-pressed John had ever been within twenty miles of what he was describing. Sidmouth, for instance, that wholly unspoilt and attractive Regency watering-place, he passed off as 'chiefly a health resort. Its beauty went with the advent of Victorian and post war villadom.' At other times, an intimate personal acquaintance with a 'beauty spot' is most evident:

> Cranmere Pool. On Dartmoor, is said to be difficult to find. It is not worth finding, a dull, small puddle in a dull large bog. There is a visitor's book which makes good reading in the way of invective.

That, like the 'noble granite warehouses, block after block along the water' of Plymouth Sound, was John in his authentic voice. So too was his healthy rage at Exeter City Council for proposing to demolish their only classical church, St Paul's, 'a modest good-looking building', and allowing St Mary Major to survive and continue to wreck the cathedral close. He had even seen the light himself on an object of his own earlier blindness, for now he found Plymouth Guildhall's Grecian proportions 'almost as glorious as the arch at Euston Station'. The whole book, visually a delight at every page, was full of the author's mischievous high spirits, whether he was observing Plymouth from the top of a bus and hurling side swipes at 'The Great Worst Road in London' or remembering with malicious glee his hated tutor at Magdalen College, Oxford, and claiming that 'For mental inspiration the Editor had only to think of Mr C. S. Lewis, tweed clad and jolly, to get busy with his pen.'

An intriguing and important question remains: who brought about the stylistic transformation in the space of two years which changed the cool, condescending Betjeman of *Cornwall* into the warm-hearted, whimsical John of *Devon*? It was a cos-

metic, stylistic change, one deliberately adopted, not a personality change, and that makes it all the more interesting. He
remained in himself as socially and culturally élitist as ever,
imagining his average reader as 'a plus-foured weekender
[shades of Arthur and Trudy Bliss], someone unable to distin-
guish a fake Tudor roadhouse from a real sixteenth-century
manor'. He may have been unaware of how potent his instruction was proving, how society was growing better informed in
his shadow, but someone's example taught him to sound the
relaxed and genial entertainer.

Which author then, of the three 1935 *Shell Guides* that he
had so recently edited, had inspired him to whimsy, supersti-
tious fun, trenchant and surprising new lines of criticism and
evocative pen-portraits of atmospheric buildings and sites? Was
it Lord 'Cracky' Clonmore, heir to the earldom of Wicklow and
often John's generous host at Shelton Abbey in Ireland,
Christopher Hobhouse, the tall, conceited lawyer, loved by both
sexes, who wrote the *Derbyshire Shell Guide*, or was it Robert
Byron, *Wiltshire*'s editor and the author of distinguished books
on travel and history, a co-founder of the Georgian Group and
someone Betjeman had known well on the *Archie Rev*?

Of the three 'Cracky' Clonmore can most easily be dismissed.
His real name – William Cecil James Philip John Paul Forward-
Howard – was as attractively pompous as his personality. It is
easy to see why the British, though not the Irish, love lords. He
added Revd to his many titles before converting from Anglo-
Catholicism to Roman Catholicism, and it was his keen church-
manship which brought him and John together. He was devoted
to work with the poor and the downtrodden. What they had to
put up with in the process can be judged by one of his classic
observations to Betjeman: 'I think that you and I are better at
understanding slum people than men who are more normal and
saner. It is not really anything to be proud of, but the way one is
made.' In giving him *Kent* to compile John must have been
trying to repay a heavy debt of gratitude for the many kind-
nesses and generosities of the past. An authentic heir to an Irish

earldom with a large Georgian Gothic house in good country ranked high in John's social register.

Unfortunately there is no evidence that Cracky could write. Much of *Kent* is taken up with essays by other writers: 'Kent and Sussex Borders' by Sheila Kaye-Smith, 'The Invasion of Kent' (by hop-pickers) by Miles Sargent, 'Rochester Cathedral' by the Dean, 'Charles Dickens and Kent' by Arthur Waugh. Lord Clonmore contributed an essay on Canterbury Cathedral and the gazetteer. The Kaye-Smith essay was predictable stuff – 'the wise motorist will not content himself with visiting Rye and Winchelsea. Inland the country is rural England at its loveliest' with 'pippin-red farmhouses' and 'white-topped oasts'. The Dean of Rochester was worse. Instead of confronting the lumbering, disjointed ugliness of his cathedral as the new John might have done, he claimed depressingly that 'a short time spent looking at it carefully reveals an interest, historical, architectural and human, which places it high among our great English churches'.

The Dean could be forgiven his lack of inspiration. Of Canterbury the highest praise that Clonmore could muster was that 'to travel in Kent without visiting Canterbury, is rather like eating plum pudding without brandy butter'. The cathedral's glass had suffered from the Puritans, 'however some good stuff remains'. Reading this no one would have guessed that several of its windows rival the very best in Chartres. He seems not to have noticed the enormous shadows of the crypt, a second cathedral within the other's belly, but instead notes that 'during the last few years, striking improvements have been made'. None, however, was listed. At Brasted, having quoted the tomb inscription of Chief Justice Heath – SUADELA POTENS, URBANITATE AUREUS, PATIENTIA FERREUS – without of course offering a translation, he added infuriatingly, 'One knows plenty of people who might take this to heart.' Then he illustrated a peer's common touch with the people of the slums in his description of Margate by advising, 'if you attend some of the pierrot performances etc., you will be surprised at their wit, humour and originality'.

Betjeman is unlikely to have improved his style by editing *Kent*, but it serves as a reminder of the artificiality and humbug of his Oxford friends that he had still to leave behind. A good seven-eighths of the new poems which he was writing at this time, and which would appear in 1937 in *Continual Dew*, prey upon themes of religious sectarianism: High and Low Church practices, *Crockford's Clerical Directory* and worldly clergymen, hymns, incense, Calvinism and death. His notorious appeal for friendly bombs to come and fall on Slough, five years before the Germans obliged, made evident his continued 'Georgian' disgust with modern reality, but 'Love in a Valley', a poem in the same collection, proved the exact opposite provided he could become engaged with the demure middle-class suburbia of Surrey and the Coulsdon woodlands. Council estates and average High Streets were still beyond the range of his sympathy.

If *Kent* was so clearly uninspiring, what of *Derbyshire*, foreign territory for a Londoner like Betjeman? Christopher Hobhouse was a formidably impressive defender of its alien beauty. An outdoor man, a tremendous walker and a devoted angler, he was also a more than competent historian and scholar who had already demonstrated a firm grasp of the politics of 1680–8 and the Glorious Revolution, and of the rise of the Cavendishes of Chatsworth. Such knowledge might well have awed John whose own grasp of history remained more emotional than factual. Surprisingly Hobhouse showed no strong interest in the architecture of the great houses whose family histories he handled so confidently. The visual impact of the *Derbyshire Shell Guide* is predominantly one of landscape with wonderful double-page spreads of Monsal Dale, the countryside of Litton and Beresford Dale punctuating the text at frequent intervals. By quoting Dr Johnson's verdict on Kedleston – 'It would do excellently for a town hall' – Hobhouse cleverly implied his own opinion. The enchanted Little Castle of Bolsover got barely a mention, Tideswell church and Derby Cathedral hardly featured.

Where Hobhouse was most impressive and where he could have influenced Betjeman was in his receptiveness to industrial landscapes:

> Everybody with an eye for form must love a railway cutting; the slick line of a slag heap is perhaps an acquired taste [but one Hobhouse had obviously acquired and, therefore, his readers might also, or so the implication ran] but there can be no question about the charm of the discreetly busy little quarries and mills, some of the latter are architectural marvels . . . they have an air of immemorial usefulness.

Derbyshire was one of the great *Shell Guides* and John, who could not yet master such literary precision, was its editor and could not help being influenced by it. But it is not easy to find in its harsh, masculine directness anything closely related to the mood of *Devon*. Hobhouse ended uncompromisingly with a complex panorama of a huge quarry threaded with mineral lines in Clee Dale, pressing his message home with the claim that these were 'typical as are any of the "beauty spots", and tend to improve, rather than detract from, their surroundings'. If, one feels, there had been any Bauhaus-style ventures in Derbyshire, then Hobhouse would have lauded them. Unfortunately there are none.

We are left then with Robert Byron's *Wiltshire*. Byron was a friend of Betjeman, though not a close one; not for him a saucy nickname like 'Bog', 'Li' or 'Dear Old Thing'. But he had effected a first introduction between Penelope Chetwode and her future husband and he had been a respected contributor to the *Archie Rev* with articles of the traditional kind, Greek and Byzantine remains, Persian mosques and Indian temples. He could be described as being, on the surface, a staid, establishment architectural historian, but one connected with another and more louche set of bachelors like Harold Acton and Brian Howard. Though dignified and even self-important he had a strong civic sense.

One of Betjeman's near neighbours, Lord Berners of

Faringdon House, a whimsical artist with a taste for the surreal, provided a wild collage of traction engines, merry-go-rounds and labourers for the *Wiltshire* cover and Byron laid out the contents with the precision of a military campaign. First came the 'Face of Wiltshire' then 'Antiquities' in order: Pre-Christian, Saxon, Norman, Later Mediaeval, Tudor, Seventeenth Century, Georgian, 'White Horses' and 'Moral'. Industries, Nature Notes, War and Sport followed and then, at last, the gazetteer.

Byron himself wrote the introductory essays, but though his judgements were sometimes quite memorable he was hopelessly pompous. Deliberating on the Angevin tympanum at Malmesbury Abbey he allowed that 'the perspicacious visitor may discover an affinity with Epstein and other modern stone carvers. He will not be wrong.' At Longleat he found 'that combination of splendour, repose and unadvertised resources, which is peculiar to our island and which has nourished so many of the islanders' most individual characteristics'. Charles II had described the Double Cube Room at Wilton as 'the best proportioned room he knew. Charles II was not untravelled. Nor is the present writer. And the latter can only say of this room that in all Europe he has seen none to compare with it.' That was easily his most inflated judgement, the kind of remark that makes Frenchmen shrug with despair: insular smugness incarnate. But he did quote an interesting French opinion describing 'English cathedral architecture as mere plumbing', one which always comes to mind when I am trying to be fair to Salisbury Cathedral. In his social concepts Byron should have been a Victorian. One dreadful photograph in his guide illustrates a theatrical old gaffer with the caption: 'A figure rarely to be seen in the countryside now is the old type of farm labourer complete with smock and mutton-chop whiskers'. The gaffer also has a wooden yoke over his shoulder to carry milk churns and is as relevant to 1930s Wiltshire as a Beefeater to modern London. In similar style, he recalls, with an air of regret, that 'Ten years ago a fiddle still accompanied the evening service' in Inglesham church.

The gazetteer, the real heart of any guide, was left to Edith Olivier, probably more a confession of ignorance than of indifference on Byron's part. Edith was 61 when she wrote the entries. A remarkable, vibrant woman who knew everyone in Wiltshire worth knowing, gravitating instinctively towards men of what in those days might be described as an indeterminate sexuality, she lived in the Daye House, a romantic retreat in the grounds of Wilton House. She also kept up an intensely warm, maternal relationship with the artist Rex Whistler who looked to her, rather than to his real mother, for comfort, advice and hospitality. During the war she would serve as Mayor of Wilton.

Here, clearly, is Betjeman's perfect model. Informed and allusive, engagingly devoted to the supernatural (where *Devon* has pixies her *Wiltshire* specializes in ghosts), Edith Olivier was able to condense her impressions into one intense, unpunctuated entry. Her Bowerchalke abounds in legends of ghosts and goblins. She cites an entry in its 1882 parish magazine on Mr Henry Good 'who loved Milton and *Hudibras*, played several instruments in a musical club which he established at the Compton Hut and, wearing his Beehive helmet and his suit of canvas quilted with wool, led many a poaching party hunting the deer in the Chase'. For Amesbury she devised another compression in a natural journalese to which Betjeman would have responded appreciatively:

> Gay's sparkling Duchess of Queensbury lived here, and Gay is said to have written the 'Beggar's Opera' in a curious grotto built into the great earthwork of Vespasian's Camp which borders the Park on one side, the Inigo Jones gateposts and some late 17th cent. garden lodges give character to the outer aspect of the Abbey domain.

Why complain that the lodges were not actually late seventeenth century but much earlier when she has drawn so much allure into so few lines? And in one extraordinary sentence she dealt with Boscombe:

Was the home of the judicious Hooker: here he wrote his
'Ecclesiastical Politie', here his sermons won him such fame that
he enlarged the church to hold his congregation by building a
single transept on the north side of the nave: the church is almost
as he saw it, though the pulpit and the old pews are 17th cent.; but
in Boscombe Church it is possible to realise what an English village
church really looked like in the days of Queen Elizabeth and
Charles I: Hooker's old rectory stands hard by the church, haunted
by the ghost said to be of an even earlier time than the venerable
writer himself: strange that his peaceful spirit could not exorcise
the restless ghost of the murderer.

Strange indeed that such a suggestive scribbler never made a
wider reputation as the authoress of passionate historical
romances. At Avebury 'the traditional Beckhampton avenue has
not yet been recovered, though it was seen standing, some
twenty years ago, by a clairvoyante'. And so she rattles away.
Wiltshire, a county whose northern half is in reality as dreary
and flat as south-west Oxfordshire, comes vividly to life. Like all
the best *Shell Guides*, *Wiltshire* teaches painlessly and
efficiently and entertainingly. John took the lesson. Through
dire hauntings, poaching on Cranborne Chase, Gay penning
music in a grotto and popular Elizabethan preachers, we are led
effortlessly into an informed awareness of the fabric of English
history and the valuable complexity of its multi-layered landscape. Without that awareness what is our own identity? It seems
a reasonable question to ask.

In the same year as *Devon* came *Somerset*, an indifferent performance by the Quennells, Peter and his father, on an elusive
and disparate county, and Paul Nash's *Dorset*, artistically the
most experimental and memorable of all the *Guides*, drama-
tized with the author's water-colours but as personable and
winning in its text as John's *Devon*. In 1937 there followed
Buckinghamshire, *Hampshire* and *Northumberland and
Durham*. *Hampshire* was brilliantly eccentric – it actually had a
photograph of the 'ghost' of a monk at Beaulieu – and tried to
break the mould by going entirely alphabetical from the first

page to the last. *Northumberland and Durham* was a grave editorial mistake, a typical piece of southern arrogance: 'the northern counties cannot be civilized enough to stand on their own, but two squashed together might make up a fairish whole'. Much later it would have to be replaced by a single book for each county, but the damage was done. The North was never conquered by Shell as the South was; indeed Yorkshire, of all counties, was never covered at all.

John Piper's superb *Oxon* came out in 1938. By that time the fee for writing a *Shell Guide* had only gone up to fifty guineas, a reminder of the pre-war stability of the pound. Ten guineas were allowed for expenses and a photographer was on offer for a month free of charge. Piper took almost all the photographs himself and rightly claimed that his labour was worth £500. Nash's *Dorset* was eerily strange in its illustrations, but Piper's *Oxon* was the definitive article in the interaction of text and photographs and line drawings, white on black. A copy is a bibliophile's treasure.

Of the seventeen purple photographs in Stephen Bone's *West Coast of Scotland*, which came out in the same year, the less said the better. Headed 'Highland Life and Scenery' they were one Betjemaine whimsy which did not come off. He intended the purple to suggest Scottish heather, but the effect was one of unstable yoghurt and it damaged the overall impact of Bone's clever and serious evocation of a Celtic territory, the old Dalriada of islands and coastal lochs, visually lovely but shattered by past history and twentieth-century unemployment. On one side of each page ran the gazetteer and alongside it a series of lessons on the Clearances, Clegs, Climbing, Sea Serpents, Crofters, Heights of Mountains and the Northern Lights. As successors to Edith Olivier's ghosts and Betjeman's pixies there was the Cailleach Bheir: 'blue black face, one eye, rust-red teeth ... if you meet in Lochaber a huge and repulsive woman gutting fish by a stream it is probably the Cailleach', and the Each Uisge or Water Horse. This sometimes appeared as a handsome young man proposing love to unwary girls who, if they did not notice his hoofs in time, got taken away to the loch and eaten. Betjeman must have loved this particular *Shell Guide*; bagpipes played 'five grace notes between two beats in a bar . . . virtuosi have played eleven before now'. It should have been followed up by three more dealing with the other three sub-kingdoms: Strathclyde, Pictland and that lost extension of Northumbria which included Edinburgh, but war was coming. In 1939 only Anthony West's *Gloucestershire* came out. Piper and Betjeman were working on *Shropshire*, which would be delayed until 1951, but by then the rival Pevsner series was beginning to appear and the whole impetus of the *Shell Guides* was fatally lost.

CHAPTER FOUR

Nikolaus on the Edge of an English Identity

Nikolaus Pevsner arrived in Birmingham during the winter of 1933 to become a paying guest for the next two years at 35 Duchess Road, Edgbaston, the home of Miss Francesca Wilson, a history teacher at Edgbaston Church College for Girls. It was not his first visit. He had been in England once before, in 1930, but on a happier occasion. On the strength of his doctorate and publications on Italian Mannerist painting he had been appointed as a lecturer in the History of Art and Architecture at Göttingen University, but then made English art his specialism. So in 1930 he came over to familiarize himself personally with a subject he had already been teaching for two years. Throughout his long academic career he was to show a talent for identifying a gap in studies and then industriously absorbing the necessary information to fill it. Marlite Halbertsma's article on Pevsner and Pinder published in *Apollo* in February 1993 has clarified Pevsner's stylistic odyssey in his last German years. On that 1930 visit he must have been intending to imitate Wilhelm Pinder's work on the German-ness of German art with an analysis of the Englishness of English art. This he delivered – 'Das Englische in der Englischen Kunst' – in 1931, an early sign of his belief that all artists are to an extent trapped in the art-forms of their native country and in the *Zeitgeist*.

This, if considered critically, is not one belief but two, and the two are liable to contradict each other. English art may easily be in one insular phase while the *Zeitgeist* (however defined) is in another. In 1714, for instance, while Europe was cheerfully relaxing into the Rococo, England sternly set its face towards the Palladian with its repetitive disciplines and its grudging staccato details of ornament. Wilhelm Pinder would have understood this phenomenon of parallel cultural contrarieties and sympathized with it. He called it, in impressive German compound terms, 'Ungleichzeitigkeit des Gleichzeitigen', but it is not clear that Pevsner had Pinder's breadth of vision.

Throughout his creative life Betjeman changed gurus as often as he bought new suits. 'Cracky' Clonmore one year, 'Huffy' Hope the next, Shand and Etchells in the early Thirties, John Piper in the last years of the decade. His inconsistency was a kind of strength: the self-confidence to admit a mistake and move on. Pevsner had one guru only, Wilhelm Pinder. It was Pinder who had been Pevsner's doctoral supervisor at Leipzig, and for the rest of his life Pevsner continued loyally to admire his old master, ignoring the fact that Pinder's insistence upon the unique character of German art made him highly acceptable to the Nazi party. He spoke at their Leipzig rally in 1933 and wrote an encomium for Hitler's fiftieth birthday in 1939.

According to Pinder's theory of parallel cultural variations an older generation of artists might be pursuing one stylistic extreme, for instance historicism in the Victorian sense, while the younger generation were experimenting daringly with an opposite concept such as Bauhaus minimalism. Pinder in fact admired the Bauhaus as an essentially German expression of design, something which did not endear him to the Nazi establishment, but his reputation as a brilliant patriotic lecturer and popularizer of art to the masses allowed him to get away with that minor heresy.

Understandably, Pevsner came to England in some degree of philosophic disorientation which he never completely overcame. He admired the Bauhaus because Pinder had admired it, but he never pressed convincingly for the younger generation of English architects to develop their essentially English version of the Modern Movement, something which could stand alongside Perpendicular Gothic and Georgian terraces as another uniquely insular episode in the long history of English design. It is also doubtful whether Pevsner was able to distance himself sufficiently from the English architectural scene to enjoy the parallel creativity of the older, but still practising, generation of English architects. As an outsider, which is what he always was, he merely encouraged a general international modernism best described as the 'Un-Englishness of English Art'. Generations are supposed to be circumscribed by thirty-year periods, so in his later years Pevsner may have seen it as correct, by Pinder's precepts, for the pendulum of style to swing back to the half-concealed historicism of the preservation groups, one of which, the Victorian Society, he incongruously chaired for many years despite his distaste for most things Victorian apart from nineteenth-century achievements in engineering. There remains, too, the paradox that Pevsner, cast out from Germany for his Jewishness, continued to admire a notably racist theorist of architectural history.

Pevsner's own time was that of the great diaspora of Jewish intellectuals from Germany once Hitler and the Nazi party came to power in 1933. Göttingen dismissed him for racial reasons at the end of that summer term, despite the fact that both Pevsner and Lola, his half-Jewish wife, were Lutheran Christians. To say, however, that he took refuge in Birmingham would be to over-dramatize the situation, for he left his wife and children in Germany, to be brought over once he had found a permanent post. He must have had good academic contacts in England for he did some lecturing at the Courtauld Institute in London during the winter of 1933–4, and he may have taken preliminary soundings at Birmingham to be assured of a sympathetic reception later in the university. A fellow-lecturer at Göttingen, an Englishman and the brother-in-law of Miss

Francesca Wilson, had recommended him to the house in Duchess Road. Miss Wilson had undertaken relief work in the 1914–18 war and continued to do so after the war in Russia, Austria and Serbia. Other refugees – White Russians, German Socialists and German Jews – had already found a refuge with her in Edgbaston. Miss Constance Braithwaite, a lecturer in the university's Social Studies Department, was also a guest in the house and it was she who introduced Pevsner to Philip Sargant Florence, Professor of Commerce and Chairman of the Social Studies Committee. As a result of their meeting Pevsner was given, early in 1934, a short-term appointment as a research assistant in the Department of Commerce. This was an unusual position for an art historian, but in those years there was much sympathy in Birmingham University for the predicament of Jewish intellectuals, and efforts were made to fit them into academic roles not always entirely appropriate to their backgrounds.

As adaptable and assiduous as ever, Pevsner made the most of his position in Birmingham, then at the hub of British industry, flinging himself into the research which was to result, in 1936, in *Pioneers of the Modern Movement* and, in 1937, in *An Enquiry into Industrial Art in England*. It must have been while he was on a round of interviews of managers and employers for the second of these two publications that he met Gordon Russell, his future employer. Russell, ten years Pevsner's senior, was a designer with a strong Cotswold Arts and Crafts pedigree, a member of the Art Workers' Guild and based at Broadway. He was a profound believer in handwork yet at the same time a most articulate champion of designing for the machine: 'There is a job for the hand and a job for the machine.' As the Managing Director of his own furnishing firm, Gordon Russell Ltd, he was able in 1935 to make Pevsner his fabrics buyer and quality controller at a salary of £500 a year. This was exactly £100 more than the salary which Betjeman had just given up at the *Archie Rev* to go freelance. That same year Pevsner moved to Hampstead Garden Suburb where he stayed for six months with

Quaker friends, John and Dorothy Fletcher, applying mean-while for British nationality, then a five-year process. Uta, his eldest child, stayed with him for a time while he looked around for a home of his own. In 1936 he rented for ten shillings a week a quite aggressively ugly Victorian house in Wildwood Terrace on the Golders Green edge of Hampstead Heath. There Lola and the two boys, Dieter and Tomas, joined him in what was to be Pevsner's home for the rest of his life. Uta continued to return to Germany during the holidays but was caught there when war broke out in 1939. Nevertheless she survived the perils of those terrible years living with her half-Jewish mater-nal aunt who was married to an academic, and then settled back happily with her family at Wildwood Terrace at the end of the war.

While Pevsner soon acquired a reputation for efficiency in Russell's firm he continued to see himself first and foremost as an academic with an eye for openings in his chosen field. Already, in July 1934, one had been offered, quite inadvertently, by Betjeman's ill-chosen guru, P. Morton Shand. That month Shand began what he intended as a grandiose series of articles in the *Archie Rev* tracing the origins of the Modern Movement in European architecture from Sir John Soane to Walter Gropius. Shand promised his readers three groups of articles, though he was to give up less than half-way through the second group. First would be Gropius to Behrens, next Behrens to Ruskin and lastly Ruskin to Soane. This was precisely the canvas that Pevsner was soon to cover in his *Pioneers of the Modern Movement*. There was, however, one disastrous difference. Shand, with characteristic perversity, chose to write his history in reverse order, starting with Gropius and working crabwise back to Soane, a ridiculous and impractical scheme that can only be explained by his eagerness to begin with his German heroes. After reading a very few articles Pevsner must have realized how much better qualified he was than this enthusiastic, but basically amateur, Englishman to unfold a predominantly European saga, starting sensibly at the beginning and concluding logically at the end with the triumph of the Modern Movement. It would be his intellectual passport into the thin and, at that time, academically unqualified, ranks of British architectural historians, and also on to the columns of the influential *Architectural Review*.

Where Nazi Germany was concerned the *Archie Rev* was, like so many organs of the British establishment, still sitting on the fence, hoping for the best. Back in October 1933, while Betjeman was still thinking of himself as the acting editor, there had been a three-page photographic feature captioned 'Architecture of the Nazis'. Alongside photographs of trim Bavarian post offices, Paul Ludwig Troost's streamlined neo-classical proposals for a House of German Art at Munich, and Pinner and Grund's suggested Modernist extension to the Reichsbank in Berlin, was Albert Speer's Chief Speaker's Platform for the National Labour Day celebrations that year on the Tempelhofer Feld. A brief editorial text, unsigned, advised readers that 'the idea of individual leadership is given great prominence in German political life today', which was a classic understatement, and that 'In the Nationalist Socialist Party today there are Kulturorganisationen Departments and official bodies, and the chiefs of these bodies are expected to function not as officials only but as "spiritual pastors and masters" to the rank and file.' In a forlornly hopeful afterthought the anony-mous editor added: 'We have heard it said that the Nazi school of architects are setting up our current English architecture as an example. That is probably true.' By 'current English' the writer, who was quite possibly John, may have meant heavy, neo-classical banks by Lutyens and Herbert Baker, that Edwardian imperial style still in the 1930s dear to the hearts of City managing directors. That was the tone of the magazine which Pevsner had to infiltrate and impress, and Morton Shand's was the level of scholarship and critical analysis that he had to excel at.

Pevsner would have seen, after reading only the first few monthly episodes of Shand's history, that all he needed to do to improve upon it would be to trace clearly how turn-of-the-century painters had given a lead and an inspiration to the architects of the Modern Movement by their concentration upon essential patterning and to give the English players – Pugin, Ruskin, Morris, Mackmurdo, Mackintosh and Voysey – their fair share of praise. This was something which the Germanophile Shand was temperamentally incapable of doing. Then, of course, it would be helpful to start at the beginning, with the Great Exhibition of 1851, and work forwards rather than opening with Gropius and a vague intention of writing back to Soane. Shand was so besotted with German influences that he actually described a typical Georgian terrace house as a 'London Reihenhaus', and, rather than refer to open-plan designs, spoke of 'Raumgestaltung' with pseudo-sophisticated relish. Once he had traced backwards through his first heroes – Gropius, Behrens, Henry Van de Velde, Adolf Loos, Otto Wagner and Hendrick Berlage – the prospect of wading through the British Victorians for several months was so dismaying that he gave up, claiming that 'the styleless rationalisation of architectural forms' had already been achieved by the late Georgians, and so a historian could leap directly from Loos back to them. It was Shand who gave Betjeman that awed respect for the Regency so apparent in *Ghastly Good Taste*. Shand believed that the Regency invented the bow window, had 'a horror of ornament' and disliked display – a strange series of half-truths. Ruskin had, he considered, done great harm to architectural progress by insisting upon an element of 'poetry' in design. Morris in turn had 'preached a Renaissance of decoration', a false move which achieved some slight freedom in the planning of a house, but virtually nothing in 'traditions of form', only 'the Fleur du Mal of the Gothic Revival in its neo-Mediaeval hot-house'.

Shand reserved his deepest mistrust for Charles Rennie Mackintosh's wife, Margaret Macdonald, his evil genius, referring casually to 'the florid coarseness of her wholly inferior decorative talent and a firm insistence on "me too" that too often led him into an uxorious ornamental vulgarity'. For a man who had married four times Shand's response to husband and wife partnerships was revealing. It has always to be remembered that he was the older, infinitely more experienced and worldly figure who had been influencing Betjeman for the last four years, not only in how to conduct a courtship and which girl to marry, but in all the perspectives of nineteenth-century art and architecture.

Shand's ridiculous articles were pouring out as late as March 1935, the year when J. M. Richards became the *Archie Rev*'s deputy editor, bringing a more informed and sensitive direction to the magazine. It would not be until January 1938 that John Piper would begin to write for it and bring an educated artist's eye to the evaluation of everything architectural of whatever function, period or style. Piper would re-educate Betjeman out of his Shand prejudices and release his natural, genial openness to the world. That much is well known, indeed their partnership is almost a cultural cliché. What is equally interesting, but far more obscure, is the extent to which Piper influenced Pevsner. For over the next few years, the two men wrote some of their most perceptive work, often in the same monthly numbers of the magazine.

Pevsner's *Pioneers of the Modern Movement from William Morris to Walter Gropius* came out in 1936 with an apparently innocent but actually rather provocative disclaimer in the Foreword. Pevsner wrote,

> I did not know of P. Morton Shand's excellent articles in the *Architectural Review* of 1933, 1934, 1935 until I had almost finished my research. The fact that his conclusions coincide in so many ways with mine is a gratifying confirmation of the views put forward in this book.

Given Pevsner's interests and the *Archie Rev*'s prestige it is difficult to believe that he had missed a single issue of the magazine since he first settled in Britain. That Foreword must have acted like a red rag to a bull as far as Morton Shand was concerned, and it was almost inevitable that he would review the book as sourly as possible for the *Archie Rev.* Pevsner had become, in April of that year, a fellow-contributor, so Shand could only hint a fault and hesitate dislike. But when Pevsner openly contradicted Shand's assessment of William Morris, describing him as 'the one real forerunner of Corbusier' and claiming that 'building in his hands became an abstract art, both musical and mathematical', Shand could easily have fought back with reasoned argument. Instead, like negative reviewers of all periods, he picked upon trivia to suggest the author's general unreliability on major matters. Pevsner's foreign origin and implied inferiority were emphasized. His English 'might be better', which was true enough, and he had failed in his choice of what might now be called U and non-U vocabulary: 'Dr Pevsner's English revisors allowed the familiar "cruet" to be called "a condiment set".' He had dated Adolf Loos's house in Geneva wrongly, it should be 1904 not 1910 (in fact Pevsner was right and Shand wrong on this point); and in one memorably vacuous put-down Shand regretted wistfully that 'oddly enough he does not even mention the Javanese influence on [the Dutch-Indonesian] Toorop'.

He must, nevertheless, have been shaken by the sheer professionalism of Pevsner's work, its confident range of continental reference, its unstinted praise for, and even bias towards, English and Scottish protagonists of the Modern Movement, and the masterly way in which he wove together the threads of art and architecture. As a teaching tool the book was irresistible, abundantly justifying its reissue in 1960 as *Pioneers of Modern Design*. Those who never heard Pevsner lecture in person can recreate his voice and his pace by reading *Pioneers*. It is direct, simple in expression and hugely confident.

It was that confidence, that disturbingly missionary zeal, which occasioned David Watkin's counter-attack on Pevsner's certainties in his 1977 *Morality and Architecture*. The passage always quoted against Pevsner is taken from the penultimate page of *Pioneers* and is certainly unfortunate if it is read with hindsight and in the light of the 1939–45 war. In a rhapsody over Gropius's model factory for the Werkbund Exhibition in Cologne of 1914, Pevsner, after comparing the building to the works of Brunelleschi, Alberti and Michelangelo, allowed that 'warm and direct feelings' in design were outdated, but that

> the artist who is representative of this century of ours must needs be cold, as he stands for a century cold as steel and glass, a century the precision of which leaves less space for self-expression than did any period before.

That was not, with so many individualists around in the media, all desperate for a little 'self-expression', a tactful conclusion to Pevsner's argument. Dr Watkin delivered a witty and perceptive demonstration of the deliberately decorative, non-functional nature of Gropius's transparent, strictly symmetrical circular staircases. But it is only necessary to read on to Pevsner's very last paragraph in the book to see why he thought his century 'cold as steel'. That was how it had, in 1933, proved for him in his expulsion from Göttingen. We lived, he declaimed sadly, in 'a world of science and technique, of speed and danger, of hard struggles and *no personal security* [my italics]'.

Of all Pevsner's many publications, *Pioneers* is the most personally revealing, the book written when he was most vulnerable to argument and change, nearer than he would ever be again to that openness which was Betjeman's most valuable and endearing quality. *Pioneers* was a polemic, but one written to include uncertainties and even arguments against its main thesis of the irresistible forward march of an impersonal, functional architecture of the *Zeitgeist*. Very soon after its publication Pevsner would, like Betjeman, be brought face to face, personally as well as in written accounts, with the revolutionary topographical perceptions of John Piper. If these had been accepted with all their subtle aesthetic and social dissection of English architecture – its complexity, the infinite value of the apparently unimportant, and the real constituents of a human landscape – then Pevsner would have become, not in a legal sense, but in his own informed awareness, English and not German. And he would have had to rewrite his *Pioneers*.

Some aspects of *Pioneers* are best passed over quickly. Pevsner's insistence that William Morris was a true pioneer of the Modern Movement can only have been tactical, a move to flatter the susceptible English art-buffs. He claimed that Morris was a pioneer of the art of the machine even while admitting that he detested and mistrusted machine art and had fought vainly against it all his life. Reduced to its essentials Pevsner's claim is as unconvincing as that. Later he tried to strengthen his case by urging that Morris revived the application of art to industrial design; but given Pevsner's own ingrained suspicion of ornament, that remains unconvincing. At the end of his long, crystal-clear analysis of the formative role of artists in shaping Modernism, he suddenly and unexpectedly turned to savage Picasso, Kandinsky, Expressionism in general and Cubism in particular. History, Pevsner thundered, will decide against the Cubists, 'their extreme individualism is of the past', an outdated élitism: 'Only in so far as their art can be regarded as decoration in the service of architecture, do they work for a new ideal, the ideal of their own century.' The mind which could come to such an arrogant conclusion can be understood, not through his analysis of architecture, where his insistence on function is consistent and often quite persuasive, but in his analyses of art where, like most of us, he is engagingly unbalanced and most unwisely revealing.

For Pevsner the Post-Impressionists were vastly superior to the Impressionists. 'The charm of Renoir's *Baignade* lay in the play of rosy young bodies', but Cézanne's *Baignade* on the other hand scorned sexual allure and was 'without any sensuous appeal . . . Cézanne does not care for the individual, he speculates on the idea of the Universe.' It was not 'quick observation of natural facts' that made an important painting, 'but their perfect translation onto a plane of abstract significance'. The Impressionists such as Renoir, Manet and Monet had given in to 'the dangerous charm of superficial beauty'. What was more valuable was 'the expressiveness of pattern'. Cézanne's women bathers echoed by their sloping backs the slant of the trees behind them. Diagonals met with 'the four main horizontals of the painting': a typical art lecturer's insight, initially impressive, basically unimportant.

As a last focus for his chapter on art as the director of architecture, Pevsner featured Edvard Munch's *The Scream* of 1893 (or as he called it, *The Cry*). Munch had wholly rejected 'superficial beauty'. Even the sex of its central figure was uncertain, but because the scream shaped the face 'it pervades the whole picture, carried by visible waves of sound' – the unity of pattern again. Pevsner concluded, 'So Munch achieves his symbolical expression of the oneness of the Universe.' This assumption of the unity of all things and the mere making of that point justified the painting. For Pevsner, Munch was 'one of the strongest, sanest and least sophisticated painters of the present day'. Similarly 'le Douanier' Rousseau, 'by his apparently helpless technique . . . has come nearer to the world of the savage than Gauguin with his superior knowledge of art'. The implication is obvious. It is desirable to be unsophisticated, to come near to the savage and to express 'the oneness of the Universe'. But Pevsner makes these claims without the slightest attempt to justify them morally or even aesthetically. Was it the Germany he had so recently fled that justified his pessimism? The Belgian Expressionist James Ensor had painted hideous masks on his revellers, not out of a sense of fun, Pevsner decided, but as 'an expression of demoniac villainy', a 'back to fundamentals'. Pevsner never quite says that he agrees with Ensor that 'the ultimate fundamental to be reached is the baseness of human nature', but that is what he implies by his illustration.

The nihilism behind that benign, bespectacled scholarly face, familiar from the dust-jackets of so many *Buildings of England* volumes, is more openly expressed in his praise for Seurat's *Grande-Jatte*. After an expert account of how Seurat endeavoured 'to push to its extreme the scientific principle which underlies the Impressionist dissolution of the surface', Pevsner urges that in this painting, as in Cézanne's *Baignade*, Van Gogh's landscapes or Gauguin's Tahiti girls, 'we are confronted with revolt . . . a sudden revelation of the futility of modern civilizations'. But what is remotely futile about a scene of Sunday afternoon pleasure-seekers on a Paris riverside? The figures have been rendered in 'the small solid units' of pointillism and made to look 'like puppets cut out of paper'; but this is no more than the creation of a flat pattern, something which Pevsner praises in a William Morris fabric, and not a profound analysis of human 'futility'.

Compared with the genial John, Nikolaus had every right to sense futility, demoniac forces and latent savagery around him. The relevant question is whether his unhappy, though hardly catastrophic, recent experiences justified him in praising an insistent patterning in art and a devaluing of realism, of 'rosy young bodies'. At what point does a perception of the 'oneness of the Universe' validate a denial of individuality in art and a demand for austere, functional logical architecture, 'cold as steel and glass'? What social advantage did Pevsner see emerging from a universal architecture of the *Zeitgeist* when the one country which appeared under Behrens and Gropius to have developed such an architecture so much more successfully than France or England had at the same time elected a destructive political regime, one from which Pevsner had escaped to England? Surely he should have been asking himself these questions rather than subsiding with gloomy relish into the advocacy of a style which 'leaves less space for self expression than its alternatives'.

Pevsner was no rebel isolate when he interpreted the contemporary art scene in this way. His views would have been seen then, or for that matter now, as perfectly orthodox and reasonable by most of his fellow-critics. But none of these would go on to describe and evaluate the architecture, old and new, of an entire nation, thereby setting up standards of worth for a whole generation. So it is relevant and valuable to know that such an authority believed at one level of his mind in 'the futility of modern civilization', 'the baseness of human nature', 'the ruthless scrapping of traditions' and the need for 'a genuine, universal style'. All these are limitations of a kind.

Yet a critic who finds even Cubism an outdated self-indulgence will respond most eagerly to spatial abstractions, the controlled flow of areas within and without a building. That is where Pevsner becomes emotional, almost unguarded. In an early Frank Lloyd Wright house he found 'a charm in the arrangement of differently shaped blocks and of rooms flowing into each other that cannot be described'. In the Library of the Glasgow School of Art, he believed that Charles Rennie Mackintosh had achieved 'an overwhelmingly full polyphony of abstract form . . . his *bravura* in playing with space raised him to the level of the great masters of Baroque architecture. Building in his hands becomes an abstract art, both musical and mathematical.' At least Pevsner is confident and frank about his values.

This is high praise and it suggests tantalizingly how Pevsner's critical role might have evolved in future years. At that point in the 1930s he was three years or more ahead of Betjeman in the maturity of his judgement and the shrewdness of his perceptions. Pevsner the architectural historian had kept his eye primarily on buildings. Betjeman the architectural journalist remained more interested in people. His very slim 1937 volume of verse, *Continual Dew*, contains two of his best-known poems, 'The Arrest of Oscar Wilde' and 'Slough', and also his masterly 'Death of King George V'; but apart from 'Love in a Valley' which gives a sensitive evocation of a middle-class, suburban house in Surrey, not one of the nineteen poems has anything significant to say about architecture. Religiosity was the prevailing theme as Betjeman oscillated between Anglo-Catholicism and Quakerdom, while keeping a malicious eye on Nonconformity with 'Our Padre', 'Undenominational' and 'Calvinistic Evensong'.

In the same volume his 'Death of King George V' anticipated

the future cultural direction of his country brilliantly in one line:

> Where a young man lands hatless from the air.

That single glimpse of Edward VIII, casually dressed and descending the steps of a small airliner, exemplified a whole new era – the cool, the laid-back, the informal. This was the twentieth century getting under way after the false starts of the Edwardian era and the 1914–18 war, in essence merely continuations of the Victorian. But then Betjeman's perceptions came to a halt. It was not the architecture of 'Slough' that disgusted him but the shallow lives and loose morality of its inhabitants. The Quaker in John was still writing. That was why, in his best-known line, he called 'Come friendly bombs and fall on Slough'. And in 'The Arrest of Oscar Wilde' he was not, despite his own dubious sexual record at Oxford, calling for a more tolerant attitude towards homosexuality. The poem is only a cleverly observed, whimsical joke, a comic recreation of a disastrous episode in English legal history, complete with cardboard lower-class policemen who talk music-hall Cockney:

> 'Mr Woilde, we 'ave come for tew take yew
> Where felons and criminals dwell.'

As popular poetry, not great but memorable and amusing, this was excellent but it was in no way a relevant contribution to the stylistic debate on English architecture in the 1930s. If one compares it all to the way in which Pevsner was beginning to write about particular English buildings, an impartial observer could be forgiven for believing that the future of English architectural criticism was safer in the hands of the *émigré* German than those of the native Englishman. In his 1936 *Pioneers* Pevsner gave an extraordinary analysis of Voysey's Bedford Park tower-house that contradicted most of his own most cherished theories of the way ahead for architectural design. At this strategic point in his life his English perceptions seemed to be outpacing the rigidity of his German theories.

Voysey's atypical and angular creation is dated 1891. Most commentators seize upon it eagerly as a foreshadowing of the Modern Movement in its tea-caddy proportions, horizontal lines and asymmetrical windows, hailing it as a significant pointer to the reach of its architect and to a direction almost taken. Pevsner would have none of that. First he conveyed its form, its indifference to 'sacred symmetry'. 'The skipping rhythm of bare white walls and rows of horizontal openings and the curved metal brackets connecting walls and roof' were not previews of Modernism but 'almost an anticipation of Art Nouveau', and Pevsner saw them as damaging deflections from Voysey's far more valuable personal pilgrimage of style. He dismissed these elements with some contempt: 'In Voysey's work they can be accounted for only by remembering that he had not yet found the balance of maturity when he ventured on such vagaries.' Instead of praising Voysey for the defiant geometry of his house, set in a Norman Shaw suburb of cosy gables and welcoming wooden porches, Pevsner saw the building as an aberration. Still, at this point, able to stand back from his own obsession with an international *Zeitgeist* style, he felt irritated that Voysey was being distracted by this tower-house from devising something far more important, the creation of the cottage vernacular prototype for middle-class housing of the next century. This house was a 'vagary'. What Voysey should have been concentrating on were those cat-slide roofs, comfortable, ground-hugging profiles, sloping buttresses and deep eaves of the true Voysey signature, houses which would be copied, perfectly adequately, by a hundred lesser architects and builders in every polite suburb and better-class council estate of Britain.

Pevsner is, at this point, almost on the edge of seeing his treasured Modern Movement as an irrelevance in England. As he observed, 'England led the growing Modern Movement exactly as long as it implied a revival of wholesome traditions.' So why should it have led it any longer? Pevsner was becoming English, was acquiring an insular perspective. As he admitted two pages later, Voysey's more typical houses had 'comfort, tidiness, straight-forwardness, restraint and delicacy of proportions. The bay windows, the rows of horizontal windows and the high-pitched gables are frankly reminiscent of the times of the Tudors, but nothing is pedantically copied.' There was the rub. 'Pedantically' or not, these features were copied. They were 'historicist' in Pevsner's interpretation of that term, period imitations. They satisfied the fantasy aspirations of a country comfortable with its past and, even though he was a German interloper, Pevsner could appreciate that and value Voysey's achievement. 'From the historian's point of view,' he wrote, 'it is no small feat to have created the vast majority of building carried out over thirty years and more.' If Pevsner had been alive now and able to write at the end of the century he would have had to write 'ninety years and more'. It was Voysey that England would follow, not the Modern Movement: the vernacular roofs and the Tudor gables are still going up. Betjeman previewed his century in the 'young man . . . hatless'; Pevsner previewed it in his impatience with Voysey's house in Bedford Park. If only he could have gone for his regular long walks, never less than twelve miles, in company with John Piper, not over the downs but through suburbia, arguing and laughing and absorbing twentieth-century realities instead of twentieth-century ideals, how differently the *Buildings of England* might have been written and how much more thoughtfully we might all be building.

CHAPTER FIVE

'How to like Everything': The Piper Factor

In 1936, riding the prestige of his *Pioneers*, Pevsner began to work his way on to the staff of the *Architectural Review*. He could not have expected, for all his expertise on European painting, to have moved straight in to write on Modernism. Morton Shand, in his review of *Pioneers*, had made it clear that he would defend his own position as the magazine's authority on all things modern. But since J. M. Richards had joined the editorial staff in 1935 the magazine had been showing an interest in lowly kitchen ware, and who better to write on the subject than the man who advised Gordon Russell Ltd on standards and whose *Enquiry into Industrial Art in England* was in preparation? Nikolaus was commissioned and responded eagerly with no less than seven articles in one year.

First, in April 1936, came Pevsner on 'Carpets', then 'Furnishing Fabrics' in June, followed by 'Gas and Electric Fittings', 'Fires and Lighting Fixtures' and, a little nearer to his real goal, 'Architectural Metalwork'. Next appeared 'The Role of the Architect', skilfully included though only marginally relevant, with lamps by Gropius and Behrens, cutlery by Van de Velde, and Mies van der Rohe chairs. 'New Materials and New Processes' concluded an active if pedestrian year. He was now a recognized name in kitchen ware, after a year in which

Betjeman had only contributed one dull book review, being far too occupied on Mondays, Tuesdays and Wednesdays with his public relations work at Shell Mex House editing the *Guides* and advising on the firm's image. Film reviews, broadcast talks and popular journalism were taking up the rest of his time.

Pevsner was not writing on architecture and the Modern Movement yet, but at least he had been able to get Kidderminster off his chest. Nikolaus hated Kidderminster with uncharacteristic venom. His work for Gordon Russell had involved frequent visits to that penny-plain Worcestershire carpet town with an art school that Pevsner found limp and derivative, and factories experimenting with bastardized Cubist designs executed in browns and yellows. He believed the manufacturers to be contented philistines who would sell far more carpets if they concentrated on plain colours. Ornament and pattern were never Nikolaus's special pleasure, and the heaving fronds and gaudy roses of the average Kidderminster carpet distressed him deeply. As C. S. Lewis was to Betjeman, so Kidderminster was to Pevsner. Years later, in his 1968 *Worcestershire*, he was still bracketing the town malevolently as 'uncommonly devoid of visual pleasure and architectural interest', but then, being a recorder of integrity, he devoted five interest-packed pages to the place.

Early in 1937 Pevsner contributed an uninspiring article on the Victorian designer Christopher Dresser and then he moved, deliberately, straight into Betjeman territory with yet another Voysey article, based on an interview with the old gentleman on his eightieth birthday. It seems not to have been an easy interview. Voysey was in gloomy retreat, damning the Modern Movement and claiming that his own fabrics and wallpapers had never sold well. But Nikolaus was not interested in failures. Here he had an Englishman who could be fitted, with some tactful adjustments, into his Modern Movement, so: 'For Mr Voysey's work, I think we can say already now without hesitation that it will last as the work of one of the few really great architects of the past hundred years.' Moreover, from his discovery of a world of decorative possibilities never yet touched by the great styles of the past a revolution has started ... in Mr Voysey's works we only recognise the artist loving all things he draws and enjoying the charm of the ornament into which they gradually merge.

This was Pevsner in a most uncharacteristically mellow, even sentimental, mood. His final, brief rapture on the place of ornament in a century that should be 'cold as steel and glass', made it even less typical.

There was, however, to be a coda to this enterprising venture into popular journalism. In 1941 Voysey died and the obituaries came rolling in. Betjeman wrote to his friend John Piper from Dublin on 17 March and, among paragraphs of disenchantment with Ireland and the Irish, noted that he had just completed an article on Voysey for 'Marx' (J. M. Richards, by that time the editor of the *Archie Rev*). As an early and sincere Voysey fan who had written two previous accounts of the old gentleman and inspired the 1931 Voysey exhibition at the Batsford Gallery, he would have seen himself as the natural author for a last warm appraisal. His article was not used. Nikolaus Pevsner, the enemy alien recently released from internment, supplied the magazine's tribute and farewell. There is no need to look any further for the source of Betjeman's subsequent dislike of his rival, not that he would ever have favoured a foreign interloper in a field he considered his own.

Back in the late 1930s, the Gordon Russell years, Pevsner was scenting success and finding that he had a reserve of human warmth. Arthur Mackmurdo, the founder of the Century Guild and an artist with a clear feeling for Art Nouveau, was the design link between William Morris and Voysey. He was still alive, aged 87, and living in Essex. Mackmurdo was Pevsner's next interviewee and far more rewarding than the disenchanted Voysey. 'Here is a man', Nikolaus wrote reverently, 'who in this year 1938 can say in a fatherly undertone: "She was a remarkable girl was May Morris ... I used to row her up the river."' In Mackmurdo, Pevsner had found a fellow enthusiast for exercise:

He will ask you out for a walk and talk to you of economic problems, his light blue eyes glittering, his wavy white hair blown by
the breeze, a black coat slipped on over his navy-blue shirt – the
kind of blue blouse which William Morris wore: the kind of blue
shirt which C. F. A. Voysey wears. And the shirt in this case – as in
other cases – is a profession of faith.

Would John, with a fag in his mouth and more feeling for
motor cars than long hikes, have gone down so well? And why
had he missed out on Mackmurdo in his own researches into the
period, losing a living witness to a past he admired? Pevsner not
only took his opportunities in an adopted country but wrote well
about them. Betjeman at this period, as in his *Bristol* broadcast
of 12 April 1937 for the BBC, was inclined to waffle on sentimen-
tally about retired colonels and admirals putting down their
newspapers to watch the lamps light up along the Avon Gorge.
He might, instead, have been writing lively, closely observed
accounts about buildings and places, so was he, in these imme-
diate pre-war years, going in the wrong direction? The question
depends for its answer on the whole purpose of topographical
analysis, which in the end requires an individual response. What
is worth writing about a building? Should the evaluation be
human, scholarly or aesthetic? If aesthetic, whose aestheticism,
that of Rex Whistler and the neo-Georgians – ideal and trim
and precious – or John Piper's – rough and inclusive over a wide
visual spectrum?

When their respective backgrounds are remembered –
Betjeman's Oxford and his idealization of the Regency,
Pevsner's feeling for the shadows of the Mannerist painters, his
eager response to Modernist ruthlessness – there should have
been no question as to who followed whom. It was Nikolaus who
should have opted for Piper's gritty realism and John for the traditionalist Georgian. In fact the reverse was to be the case and
Piper's own background and personality explain the paradox.
He had a head start in life, three head starts in fact. He had not
been brainwashed into cultural attitudes at Oxford or
Cambridge, having trained at the Royal Academy and the Slade;

then he had gone through the phase of being an abstract painter and had come out on the other side; and lastly he had a lovely and clever wife, Myfanwy, whom Betjeman openly, lustfully, but chivalrously, loved, just as he loved, though not lustfully, John Piper himself. They were a well-matched trio. After Piper's near perfect *Shell Guide* to Oxfordshire the two men got on so well that they decided to do a *Shropshire* together. Piper was four years older, giving him that edge of maturity over John, and the pair laughed their way around England's oddest county, neither northern nor southern, neither Midland nor Welsh, with Betjeman being cheerfully indoctrinated into Piper's way of seeing each and every building without preconceptions.

In the January 1938 issue of the *Architectural Review* Piper moved into the topographical game with razor-sharp assessments of 'The Nautical Style'. His impact proved both instant and cumulative. No one had written from quite such an anarchic, wonderfully persuasive viewpoint before. Magazines throughout the Thirties had been awash with topographical studies, some picking delicately over park landscapes and spa towns, others bewailing the spreading tentacles of ribbon development, the loss of old town centres, the curse of suburbia, all that easy apocalyptic writing of the 'Whither England?' line. The *Archie Rev* writers, Betjeman included, had been singing to the tune of the CPRE ever since Clough Williams-Ellis fired off his angry 1928 polemic against ribbon development on the country's expanding network of main roads, *England and the Octopus*. Piper's line was insidiously, thought-provokingly, different, and someone on the magazine's editorial board must have been taken by it. All through the war years, when so much was being destroyed by bombs and so many opportunities for post-war rethinking were literally being opened up, his views on the environment, some radical, others merely subtle and almost traditional, were coming out in the magazine, illustrated with rare professionalism in colour and black-and-white.

In 1938 the entire British coastline, thousands of miles of it, was interpreted in 'The Nautical Style'. Piper had perceived how the weather-battered functionalism of marine artefacts – bollards, buoys and lighthouses – had resulted in three qualities: gaiety, 'black, white and red are the colours that show up best at sea'; strength, 'a sailor never forgets and sometimes exaggerates the forces of the wicked elements'; and contrasts, 'curious structures consisting of bulbs and cones and cylinders hoisted on poles that are very authoritative and very melancholy'. These, he maintained, had infected all seaside architecture and made it 'evocative rather than decorative . . . the straightforwardness and simplicity of it is a positive example and a clean tonic'. His dashing photo-feature on Folkestone impressed his point convincingly. Then in 1939 came 'A Topographical and Critical Survey of the Bath Road', which was, in reality, a topographical and critical survey of the roadside furnishings of every main highway in Britain, only months before the war froze the whole network into suspended animation. That was the year when Betjeman succumbed completely to Piper's anarchic aesthetics, writing on Whittington Station, north Shropshire, 'The Seeing Eye', which was to be his last article in the *Archie Rev* for the duration. It was also arguably his most important, though Piper supplied its best lines as Betjeman quoted his artistic mentor at every turn in the argument. It has a second title: 'How to Like Everything', a claim which disturbed Pevsner profoundly and provoked a tardy editorial rebuke from him five years later. In the next year, 1940, with the war hotting up, Piper, now an official war artist, contributed two elegiacally subtle studies, 'A Tour of Hafod' and 'Towers in the Fens', both influential but neither revolutionary, and the most challenging of all his manifestos, 'Fully Licensed'. This was a reconsideration of the English public house and such an affront to both neo-Georgian and Modernist standards of good taste that if Nikolaus, then languishing in mild internment as a foreign alien at a camp in Huyton, just outside Liverpool, had ever got a sight of it he must have longed for a return to polemic journalism.

In 1941 Pevsner was released from token captivity, loyally

clearing debris from bombed streets, firewatching, writing his *Outline of European Architecture* and becoming active again on the *Archie Rev*, this time as a member of the editorial board now that J. M. Richards was on war work. Betjeman was safely out of the way in Dublin. He had been appointed as Press Attaché to the British Ambassador and ordered to charm pro-Axis Irishmen, which he did so ably that the IRA actually considered assassinating him. Meanwhile, a chance encounter one night during firewatching on the roof of Birkbeck College had resulted in an invitation to Pevsner to lecture to the students below, thereby initiating his long association with that institution. Soon he was also dominating the *Archie Rev* with important articles on Richard Norman Shaw, Roger Fry and the Omega Workshop, and Frank Pick and the London Underground. He had escaped from kitchen ware and was well on the way to establishment status. Piper was allowed one genteel perception on 'The Art of Cotman' in July 1942, but then came a positive fusillade of his observations: 'Rustications', 'Semicircles' and two articles on 'Colour in Buildings' in 1943, 'Blandford' and 'Warmth in the West' in 1944, 'Shops' (an extreme Piper manifesto), 'East Budleigh' and 'Colour in the Picturesque Village' in 1945. All these last nine were related studies on the surface treatments and textures of popular architecture. That *Shropshire Shell Guide*, blocked by the outbreak of war, would not be published until 1951, and for Betjeman personally the war was very ill-timed. Without its interruption the whole country would have been covered by the *Shells*, proselytized and converted by 1945 to the Piper-Betjeman way of looking at the built environment. The series would never really regain its original impetus in the post-war austerity. All three men – Betjeman, Piper and Pevsner – had good wars. Betjeman served as a guided cultural missile in neutral Ireland and Piper as a war artist, but in terms of career prospects, Pevsner's was easily the most fortunate.

His *Outline of European Architecture* had been published in 1942 and in its confident sweep, from obscure Carolingian monasteries to a detailed discussion on exactly which mid-Western architect really pioneered the first skyscraper, it established his unchallenged eminence as an architectural historian who could set British buildings in a world context. Betjeman's general opinions on Pevsner as a writer were always less than favourable. In a later letter to Jock Murray on Henry Russell-Hitchcock's Pelican History he remarked, 'His judgements are better than the Professor-Doktor's but his style is as bad. I think as soon as the specialist art-historians extend their range to cover the whole of the western world, they become unforgiveably dull.' Probably Betjeman had taken offence when Pevsner concluded his *Outline* with a damning attack on English, as opposed to American, architectural studies:

> where are the modern biographies of Hawksmoor and then of Barry, Scott, Burges, Street, Brookes, Pearson, Sedding, Voysey and so forth? . . . America is prouder of her achievements than Britain, or at least more attached to them . . . in England what attention is paid to Victorian buildings and design is still, with a very few exceptions, of the whimsical variety.

As well as being a glancing attack on Betjeman's lack of academic standards, this was an open declaration of Pevsner's intention of remedying the situation. These amateurs needed some academic rigour.

It is not easy to convey this wartime battle, not precisely of styles but of aesthetic values, in print as so much of it was waged with Piper's own perfectly aimed photographs and atmospheric sketches on one side, and the full resources of the *Archie Rev*'s layout team, those finely honed visual flatterers, on Pevsner's side. Nor were hostilities ever declared openly. But there was certainly a point, early in 1944, when Pevsner felt his own stylistic values to be so challenged that he almost changed course and had to call up the Picturesque theorists of the eighteenth century, Richard Payne Knight and Uvedale Price, to defend his position. If the debate had been held in a prosperous country at peace the vote might have gone very differently. Pevsner only won because Britain's disastrous economic situation after the war made colourless austerity and self-denying functionalism the more acceptable creed.

This was David Watkin's point in an article entitled 'Sir Nikolaus Pevsner: A Study in "Historicism"' in the September 1992 issue of *Apollo*:

> Writing in the early 1940s Pevsner seemed to revel in the harsh austerities of war-time Britain. They even provided a model for the new world which he and his fellow editors at the *Architectural Review* wished to usher in once the war was over. The story has yet to be written of the propaganda war they waged in the pages of that journal for the acceptance of the new egalitarian order and the anonymous collectivism of its drab high-rise blocks, its hatred of historic tradition, and its willing obliteration of established patterns of both environment and of living.

It was not in fact the magazine's fault that the post-war government opted to follow Pevsner's line rather than that of Piper. In the propaganda war waged within the pages of the *Archie Rev* both sides were given a very fair hearing.

To understand the libertarian Piper viewpoint, one as applicable to Piper's theory on acceptable building as to Betjeman's chosen subject-matter for poetry, it is best to begin at the end with Piper's outburst in his 'Shops' article of March 1945. Shrewdly foreseeing the banal shopping streets of a chain-store future he urged independent shop-owners to

> look to the Victorians, not for a copy book but for an example: an example that in matters of colour *it is better to be too vulgar than too nice; too fussy than too simple* . . . that marbling is still more attractive to the eye than marble veneer, that to express your taste in your shopfront, *whether it is good or indifferent taste*, is more laudable – and will ultimately attract more and better custom – than to adapt a fashion that forbids self-expression.

This declaration of aesthetic independence was backed up by his own bold colour washes of streets in Welsh towns, and by his subtle analysis of nineteenth-century house-painters. He recorded how 'their mid-purple brown looked fierce and their "light" and "dark" stone durable like iron . . . French greys and dove greys were simulations of granite.' If only his analysis of shops had been applied to post-war housing all those dull working-class estates of acceptable houses that make a suburb in the north look exactly like a suburb in the south could have been avoided. Instead there would have been the free-for-all of pre-war housing, the despair of the CPRE, that lively confusion of styles which John had scorned in his *Ghastly Good Taste* and Osbert Lancaster had mocked with negative wit. Those Spanish, neo-Georgian, Jacobean and Tudor recreations fought it out in lively variety with the occasional Modernist on every 'Drive', 'Walk' and 'Avenue' of the 1920s and 1930s. Before his conversion to Piper's aesthetics John was, in his 1937 'Antiquarian Prejudice', prophesying that 'the luckless occupants' of 'imitation Tudor and Queen Anne villas' would be 'in a few years' time saddled with a slum'. But after his enlightenment, in an appreciation of 'Bournemouth', he would relish that once despised suburbia: 'stucco Tudor-style villas', 'cheerful chintz, low-pitched roofs of local stone and broad eaves – wholesome and simple buildings like home-made cakes'. But by that time planning, good taste and standardization had become the disasters which John would have to attack. Piper's thesis was that 'good taste' was bad taste, and he made it convincingly: but after the war good taste would become firmly embedded in the hierarchy of planners, regulations and third-rate journalism.

All Piper's preceding articles had been building up to this defiance of dreary consensus. In 'Warmth in the West' he had painted and described the colour-washed houses of Devon seaside towns 'to point to striking examples of "vulgarity and provincialism" from which the unprejudiced might derive hope and profit'. But what other self-appointed arbiter of taste would ever have Piper's artistic self-confidence and make 'vulgarity and provincialism' a war cry? What must Pevsner the unpatterned have made of Piper's lengthy, lavishly illustrated 'Fully Licensed' when it urged 'that a pub is a false-fronted, painted

palace, that leads to fun or ruin', or that 'their bars very often
have, too, patterned plaster ceilings that are maligned by the too
tasteful, but [are] of good craftsmanship and a thoughtful elab-
orate design'? 'Look out', Piper directed his readers, 'for the
wonderful patterns engraved and frosted on bar doors, windows
and mirrors and regret that here again we have invented
nothing so appropriate to take their place. The birds or ships or
flowers elaborately engaged among floral scrolls produce *a
splendid artificiality'*. He had the confidence to hold up gin-
palace décor for admiration: 'there are stucco curlicues over the
portico, curlicues in pitchpine over the door inside the portico,
and then a vista, past a palm or so, of curlicues upon curlicues'.
Writing on bar fittings he pointed out that 'Good taste is out of
date before "the regulars" have got used to it . . . none of these
things must be consciously in good taste . . . they represent,
within their limitations, a vernacular tradition for whose disap-
pearance the country would be much poorer . . . the Georgian
fight is slowly turning into a victory. The Victorian one has
hardly begun.'

Did Pevsner, who later became Chairman of the Victorian
Society, blench when he read that? With his sojourn of several
years in Baroque and Rococo Dresden did he recognize in the
gin palace a true Rococo flowering? The trouble with Piper was
that he saw beauty almost everywhere, in the geometry, 'very
prominent, very authoritative and very melancholy', of har-
bourside furnishings; in unadmired towns like Reading where
'even the streets of terra cotta shops and houses in the centre of
the town have a good deal to be said for them, when you know
them in different lights'. The majority of critics and commentators depend for their substance on disliking most features of
any topography and cherishing just a few. For Betjeman, a man
of natural enthusiasm, more inclined to laugh and like people
or places than to scowl and disapprove, Piper was a revelation.
He opened up the gates of enjoyment, passage through which
made Betjeman the poet of reassurance, the positive writer
whom everyone read. That 1933 article on Leeds is proof that it

had always been John's inclination to go that way. He was a Pop
Poet before the Liverpudlians, Roger McGough, Brian Patten
and Adrian Henri, and more acceptable because he stooped from
a higher level of sophistication to observe middle-class as well
as working-class life.

Betjeman finally saw the light at Whittington Station on a
branch line, now long disused, from Ellesmere to Oswestry in
north Shropshire. John loved stopping trains and this one, in
which he and Piper were travelling, stopped there for more than
half an hour. Piper got out and sketched the stuccoed station
house with its yellow walls, heavy bargeboards and Jacobean-
style chimney-stacks. It was not, at first sight, a remarkable
building, yet it had a cheerful decorative confidence, an asser-
tive character of its own. Piper's drawing of it fronted the article
in the *Archie Rev* the month that war broke out in Europe.
Supporting Betjeman's text are six pairs of buildings, all drawn
or photographed by Piper in expressive detail, with his own
analysis of each set against imagined comments by a clergyman,
an architect and an architectural journalist, three representa-
tives of 'good taste'.

His clergyman, Mr Squinch, was a romantic medievalist. He
would have read William Morris's *News from Nowhere* and have
preferred a station 'not of barge board and stucco, but of goodly
carven stone', a building to suit an England of 'strong castles and
stately churches'. Mr Quantity, the architect, would have
advised 'the use of local stone, so as to harmonize with the
neighbourhood'. The fact that there was no local stone and that
all the houses around were red brick was lost on his doctrinaire
mind. Worst of all the trendy architectural journalist, Young
Camshaft, looked through the window spinning fantasies of the
future and saw instead of this unassuming stuccoed house, 'a
place of soaring crystal towers among spacious parks dotted
with motor cars while the sky is flecked with noiseless aero-
planes'.

Despite some unfortunate echoes of the prose style of
Thomas Love Peacock the whole compilation is, as a teaching

tool, persuasive in the extreme, pure Piper aesthetics. Whittington Station is a pleasing product of Victorian England and of 'the happy hopeful mind of the architect'. Betjeman's own summary, that Pevsner brooded over for five years, was that Piper had enlarged our visual life:

> Instead of despairing of what we have always been told is ugly and meretricious, he has accepted it at its face value and brought it to life. He has made us look a second time, without any sense of satire, moral indignation or aesthetic horror. He has done the job of an artist.

It was an appeal for critics of every description to stop using the word 'hideous' as an automatic reflex to any remotely disturbing artefact, much as they might use 'obscene' as an epithet for anything provoking an adverse moral reaction. As a sign of his conversion the new, humble Betjeman vowed, if he was spared, to emerge at the end of the war 'with a deep sense of jazz-modern [Art Deco] and a genuine desire to preserve the bogus Tudor of the new industrialism', precisely the styles that the *Archie Rev* years had conditioned him to deplore. This testament and his promise of a post-war direction of aesthetic openness he would most faithfully fulfil:

> We will have to go further than good taste, Norm and Perp, Queen Anne and the Orders and genuine modern if we are to retain our senses. By following Mr Piper, and by taking scenery as it is and not what we have been told it ought to be, we will be getting all the good we can out of the war. In any other direction madness lies.

Reading this formidable argument against doctrinaire aesthetics Pevsner for a while kept his counsel, establishing his own reputation for orthodoxy and social correctness with an innovatory and admirably researched article on Victorian tenements in London, 'Model Housing for the Working Classes'. In 1942 he dipped back shrewdly into a 1929 number of the magazine and re-presented Morton Shand's 'Underground'. Compared with Shand's prose, Pevsner's 1942 piece was tame, but it followed exactly the same lines with a precise and scholarly list of stations and their dates. Nikolaus praised Frank Pick and London Transport by making entirely conservative and traditional comparisons: 'an orderliness and unpretentious harmony have been achieved on which the eye does not tire to rest, a style as near in spirit to that of Gray's Inn, the squares of Bloomsbury, early Wedgwood coffee sets and Georgian cutlery, as our age can hope to get'. Not a hint here of Bauhaus disciplines, so was this a sincere comparison or subtle flattery of the adopted nation? It is impossible to say, but 'Georgian cutlery' and underground trains make an oddly strained duo. Perhaps he was intent on making appropriately 'English' signals. His 'Omega' was written in the same mood to prove that the so-called 'Teutonic Expressionism' of Gropius's early period, 1920, had been anticipated in England long before the war by Roger Fry's workshop, but that it was only an interesting distraction from the mainstream development between Morris and the mature Gropius. His 'Richard Norman Shaw' was contrived pointedly to re-evaluate and admire a Victorian architect whom Betjeman had casually dismissed.

As a detached outsider, but now a naturalized Englishman, he would have seen certain merits, practical and economic if nothing else, in the Piper-Betjeman proposals for appreciating the lively stylistic chaos of England's towns and countryside. At the lowest level it could be described as making the best of a bad job. So how could such formless perceptions be systematized? His solution was very clever because it was very English and carefully orchestrated from an editorial desk.

First in January 1944 came an ambitious, but by *Archie Rev* standards rather lumbering, editorial compilation, anonymous, framed as an apologia for all the various eccentric and quirky articles which had appeared in the magazine over the last few years, on cemeteries, follies, 'those townships of follies known to us as suburbs' and, casually included, Piper's article on Hafod, a romantic ruined house in Cardiganshire. All these, the compilation insisted loftily, had their place in the British landscape. 'Billy Brown of London Town', the editorial's embarrassing evocation of the man in the street, often mixed his styles but 'The fear of one's Victorian chandelier looking out of place in an Aalto environment is wholly unjustified.' So how could a democratic society 'be brought round to *the saving grace of a Bauhaus style without the application of force*? [my italics]' The extraordinary answer to that extraordinarily threatening question was 'that the Bauhaus must accept Sharawaggi'. This was a Chinese term, popular among eighteenth-century garden designers, to describe a casual asymmetrical grace in landscape, brought about by placing apparently discordant features in attractive accord. The anonymous editors (had Pevsner and Shand come together at last?) believed that what they called 'exterior furnishing' or the average, stylistically uncontrolled townscape could be saved 'by the application of Picturesque theory to the urban scene'. Pictures, they believed, 'would do more than words to convey the truth and charm of a twentieth-century Sharawaggi'.

This was how Piper's all-inclusiveness could be tamed by a tasteful mixture of disparate parts. He was named first in the roll of honour: 'Men like John Piper, Paul Nash, Edward Bawden, Eric Ravilious' ranked along with 'that great urban romantic, Richard Sickert'. When past contributors to the debate were evaluated there was praise again for 'above all John Piper's articles whose seemingly unconnected titles and manifold themes all contain the same message', a message Pevsner now claimed to have taken on board. One note of reserve, however, was sounded:

> The case is to some extent summed up in John Betjeman's 'The Seeing Eye or How to like Everything' (Vol. 86, 1939), a genial overstatement of an approach which, let it be emphasised again, accepts the modern idiom as integral to it, or rather sees Picturesque theory as an integral part of the modern idiom, the fantastical being no more than a part.

The editorial's conclusion was that 'the modern town-planner is free to pick up Picturesque theory at the point before its corruption by the Gothic Revival; pick up the theory, rediscover the prophets, and apply the principles'.

Later in the same year, 1944, Nikolaus put his name openly to 'The Genesis of the Picturesque', a perfect example of his crystal-clear lecturing style, reducing the whole of Christopher Hussey's *The Picturesque, Studies in a Point of View* of 1927 to a few pages. Sir William Temple led to Lord Shaftesbury, the *Spectator* took up the flame, Addison, Pope, Switzer and *Britannia Illustrata* followed, and lastly came Batty Langley – the genesis was complete. Nikolaus referred back to the January article on Sharawaggi and ventured his own conclusion that Alexander Pope's garden at Twickenham 'we would now call Rococo more than anything else'. He did not go on to include Piper's gin palaces as examples of the same.

He had at least made some moves away from his set position on the Bauhaus and Modernism. England was to be enticed into it by degrees. One terrible photograph in that Sharawaggi article illustrated a modern flat unit inserted into a terrace of New York brownstone houses. It was captioned, 'Witness the highly successful New York composition above. It should dispel the fallacy that discrepancy in window proportions is fatal.' Most would probably agree that it did exactly the opposite. Where the Modern Movement was concerned Pevsner could be disturbingly myopic. The most charitable interpretation of Nikolaus's proposal for an urban Sharawaggi is that he was anticipating, in 1944, the picturesque disposition of modern blocks of flats among the parkland trees of the Alton Estate at Roehampton of 1951. But that ugly little photograph of a New York street is what he really had in mind. He wanted all styles to flower together until 'Billy Brown of London Town' had grown accustomed by degrees to Bauhaus solutions.

Quite how watchfully and nervously Nikolaus hovered over his pet projects, guarding them from possible corruption, was demonstrated in the May issue of 1945. Piper was to deliver a notably seductive account on 'Colour in the Picturesque Village' in the next issue, pressing his usual theme of unfettered popular

taste triumphant. Beneath a colour illustration of East Budleigh
the editor printed helpful advice to the unwary:

> Just as the true meaning of the Gothic Revival, which at that time
> ran parallel to the Picturesque Movement, was obscured as soon as
> archaeological mutation set in, and *is only truly recovered now that
> we build with steel and glass on Gothic principles* [my italics],
> though not in Gothic forms, so the picturesque approach can only
> be really helped to-day (help against a schematic inhuman treat-
> ment of contemporary architectural problems is much needed) if
> it is taken right away from the irritation of Tudor half-timbering
> and Georgian sash and pediment, and attempted afresh, with a
> mind familiar with Uvedale Price's ideas, or instinctively sympa-
> thetic to them, but with a modern eye.

In other words: 'Thank you, Mr Piper, for your timely warning.
We in the *Architectural Review* intend to undermine it.' He
had accepted one point only – that there was a danger of dehu-
manizing city centres with arid blocks of concrete geometry.
But historicist revival styles, Tudor or Classical, were not the
solution to this problem. The solution was . . . and there he
stopped. He had no positive answer to offer, only that someone
'with a mind familiar with Uvedale Price's ideas' would come
up with something. His implication is that a variety of vertical
and horizontal units, such as Uvedale Price had urged to
improve the horizontal monotony of his contemporary Bath,
might equally save a modern Birmingham or Liverpool from a
similar monotony. All the units would, however, have to be executed according to Bauhaus structural logic and in forms of
Bauhaus simplicity. Their only relief would be a varied profile.
And that was Nikolaus Pevsner's position at the end of the war:
how could a democratic society 'be brought round to *the saving
grace of a Bauhaus style without the application of force?*' It
could be done by insidiously infiltrating historic towns and
cities with raw, new blocks of modernist design until, in the
end, the entire urban fabric could be transformed into what
Betjeman had dreaded – the Brave New World of Mr
Camshaft.

CHAPTER SIX

Bourgeois Socialism and
'Der Great Categorist'

The race to bring out the first complete series of architectural guides to the counties of England began some time before the war ended. With hindsight Betjeman should have waited until Shell became interested again in continuing the series which had faltered in 1939. But with petrol virtually unobtainable the company had, for the time being, lost interest in persuading motorists to make long, unnecessary journeys. The publishers John Murray were, however, ready to revive their *Murray's Guides*, discontinued after the First World War, and Collins was equally eager to begin another county series with colour illustrations. Betjeman disliked colour photography and felt loyal to Jock Murray, who had taken a chance by publishing his volume of poetry, *Old Lights for New Chancels*, in 1940, so he and Piper committed themselves to Murray's. The approach was to be primarily visual with generous photographic coverage. Every county in England was to be included and a concertina file was created with a holder for each county ranged alphabetically, with four extra spaces for Wales, Scotland, Ireland and the Cotswolds. Letters in the Murray archive prove that initially Marcus Whiffen was to be involved on the misunderstanding, it seems, that he had a rich resource of photographs that could be pillaged. Later Whiffen had to be eased out, Betjeman claiming that his photos made even old buildings look ugly.

John had got back from Ireland in the autumn of 1943, but before any county research could begin he became involved first in making heritage-type propaganda films for the Ministry of Information and then in hush-hush work for the Admiralty which was improbably based in un-maritime Bath. For the next thirty years he was to be constitutionally short of money to support his family, his lifestyle, his London *pied-à-terre* and his fondness for travel. So when he should have been getting on with the first county, Buckinghamshire, he was forever being distracted by efforts to make a little extra money broadcasting, producing films, working with the British Council in Oxford and writing short, popular articles for the tabloids. Piper was far more in control of his time and that might explain the unsatisfactory imbalance between illustration and text which eventually developed in the Murray *Buckinghamshire*.

Pevsner meanwhile had been making his own plans. His determination to bring order and depth to the amateurish world of British architectural writing had been apparent in that last chapter of his *Outline of European Architecture*. Before the war ended Allen Lane had been employing him part-time as the Literary Editor of the King Penguins, and Lane readily accepted his proposals for the *Buildings of England* series. The books were to be modest paperbacks, one per county, covering every building of architectural significance. It was an encyclo- paedic aim but the organization of the project was unfortunate from the start. Pevsner was as hyperactive as Betjeman, though possibly more disciplined in his work schedules. In addition to his activities on the board of the *Architectural Review* he had, since 1942, been a lecturer at Birkbeck College, an institution set up for mature students able only to follow evening courses. That should have left Pevsner free in the daytime, but he was dedi- cated to academic writing and study and, unlike Betjeman, he could not drive. So instead of going out to survey the prospec- tive ground and acquire first-hand impressions and experience he persuaded Allen Lane to fund what almost amounted to a minor research institute. Two refugee German art historians, Mrs Schilling and Miss Schapire, were employed to do research in London libraries, getting material on buildings and places, then transferring it to files for Pevsner's future use. Pevsner referred to these women as 'my slaves'. John Harris, who worked briefly alongside them in 1953, described them as 'two dear German *émigré* ladies, who might just as well have been gathering information on golf courses, for all they knew about architecture'. Armed with their pieces of paper and very little else Nikolaus aimed to produce two guides a year, one on a mild southern county after a few weeks' intensive touring in his Easter vacation, the other on a cold northern county in the summer.

It all worked like a rather expensive cottage industry, with the two part-time German researchers, a secretary and another full-time assistant. Lola Pevsner drove the car which Allen Lane had lent them. Initially this was a Wolseley Hornet, but it proved fractious and was replaced. In December 1949 Pevsner was grumbling: 'much as we liked the little Standard . . . one cannot lock up sufficient luggage, both personal and all the books and boxes of notes which I need for the job, and that means that one can never leave the car unattended'. Allen Lane told him to make the best of it and when Easter came round Pevsner wrote soothingly: 'We have the greatest trust in the little Standard and as Lola is going to do the driving, I am confident the car will not be the worse for wear, even considering Devonshire hills.' On the one occasion when Pevsner, who had managed to pass the driving-test, actually drove himself, the car received dents and scratches for the repair of which he had to pay personally. At night the Pevsners stayed in cheap hotels or bed-and-breakfast places, and lunch was a packet of sandwiches. They were perfectly satisfied. Pevsner claimed not to look at his research notes on sheets of half foolscap until after he had inspected the buildings to which they referred. The evening brought no respite. Before going to bed Nikolaus wrote up everything he had seen in the day while it was still fresh in his mind. If many, or even the majority, of his entries are uninspired notes then the pace and method of their writing are to blame. 'I beg you not to forget', he urged his colleague at Penguin, Eunice Frost, in a brief secretary-aided interlude from one of these working holidays, 'that I have to write 60,000 to 80,000 words in the course of this month, always from 7–11 p.m.; so dictating is a wonderful blessing'. Lola's reactions are unfortunately not recorded, but by that time she had been long accustomed to Nikolaus's unrelenting appetite for work. On their honeymoon in Switzerland she had found him restive after the first two days. When she asked if he had anything to read, he produced an entire file of work from their luggage, sat down and got his pen out. Thereafter the honeymoon went smoothly.

The schedule was first planned in 1945. The two rival teams, Pevsners and Betjemanites, were well aware of each other's existence. 'I don't think much of this German, do you?' was Piper's reaction in a note to Jock Murray. The two Johns had chosen to begin the *Murray's Guides* with their two home counties, Buckinghamshire and Berkshire. Pevsner was to write to Allen Lane in July 1950 to say that 'Berkshire has not yet been prepared by any of my assistants, and I have not specially pressed for it because it is one of the two Piper and Betjeman guides and we had made a vague gentleman's agreement to keep away from each other's counties for the time being', so it was not a cut-throat war. In the event Pevsner made the wiser choice. Neither of the first two *Murray's* covered popular tourist areas while the third, *Lancashire*, proved a disaster in terms of sales. Pevsner, however, had chosen one very populous county and one prime tourist coast. Even so, the first three *Buildings of England* – *Cornwall*, *Nottinghamshire* and *Middlesex* – would not appear until 1951, which should have given the rival team at Murray's a clear lead.

It is hard now, in affluent times, to reconstruct the strangely passive national mood of those straitened post-war years. The privations, the austerity, the rationing of food and clothes can be listed, and the unpainted drabness of the streets described, but what is harder to convey is the almost eager acceptance of such conditions by the general population. A government for the working class had been elected in 1945 by a huge majority as a willing continuation of the wartime spirit. The war years had pulled the whole country together in shared suffering and shared excitements. Now there was a readiness to accept a miserably low standard of life and living conditions provided that dramatic political activities were seen to be taking place. Whole industries, rail, coal, iron and steel, were nationalized, a Health Service was set up, large parts of the Empire were made independent, and impressive (and ultimately ridiculous) projects like the ground-nuts scheme in the Gold Coast were launched. Foreign currency was severely rationed, as was petrol. The aristocracy were seen to be on their beam ends and comedies were produced for theatre-goers to enjoy this amusing impoverishment. Provided that everyone seemed to be making sacrifices no one was desperately disturbed. These were the years when the destruction of the English country house went ahead and when, in cities like Liverpool, blocks of flats were rushed up for returning servicemen and their families, though they were of such a low standard that most of them had to be demolished thirty years later.

In retrospect Britain seemed to have reached a nadir but at the time, apart from the severe winter of 1947, no one was very conscious of this. Austerity was in the air and Pevsner was in his element. Friends tended naïvely to describe him as apolitical, but at heart he was a deeply committed parlour pink. Only a true socialist could have lived in and loved Hampstead yet clung tenaciously throughout his professional career to the cloudy tenets of the Bauhaus, that faith in an international working class housed in starkly functional units designed by dedicated architects. Britain's national austerity favoured cheap solutions to architectural problems, and cheap solutions tended to be logical Modernist ones. Pevsner was a Labour Party supporter for both aesthetic and social reasons. The possibility has to be weighed up that Nikolaus Pevsner, by his prestige and tacit approval, contributed at this time to some of the dreariest housing of twentieth-century Britain. It was not until 1969, in an account of tower-blocks in Manchester (*South Lancashire*), that he made that despairing comment, always quoted by his loyal apologists:

> Do we really want these towers of flats everywhere? Do tenants want them? Should they be accepted as living conditions by any but bachelors, spinsters, young couples without children and old people? Will they not be the slums of fifty years hence?

That took little prophetic insight for by that time many of them were already slums. Pevsner knew all about tenement slums; he had inspected and written about the bug-infested apartments of the working classes in the *Architectural Review* of January 1943. Between then and 1969 terrible damage would be done, visually and socially, to the towns and cities of his adopted country largely in the name of the Modern Movement which he revered and uncritically eulogized. Back in 1939, in that Whittington Station article, Betjeman had accurately forecast the tedium of a Modernist future. If an English poet and an English artist had the sensibility and the wit to envisage the horrific consequences of a cheap International Modernism back in 1939 then Pevsner, the expert from abroad, should have been able to stand back from theory and cry for caution in 1950 when those consequences were actually unfolding. But should a man with no English social background have been encouraged so quickly to a position where he could exert an unwise and, in a very real sense, an 'alien' influence?

This is a delicate point, a comment perhaps on *émigrés* in all areas of life, but possible truths need to be aired. The English, particularly those of Betjeman's generation, with the 1914–18 war a recent memory, tended to dislike and mistrust Germans. But they tended also to respect them for their power, their efficiency and their towering cultural stature. Most English are pervaded by both snobbery and xenophobia, but these two forces can, and often do, work to give foreign artists and experts a head start in this country. An inverted snobbery often projects a naturalized foreigner to high academic rank, to conduct a British orchestra or to direct a British museum. Pevsner benefited at least a little by being German-born but his advancement and his prestige carried responsibilities.

True, he offered great expertise at a time when many of his apparent English equals were mere amateurs. But an architectural historian, who could discourse on the charm of Norman Shaw houses in Bedford Park, should have been able to admit to himself the soulless monotony of buildings based entirely upon the most logical solutions to structural demands. Indeed we know that Pevsner had admitted it when he wrote that note to Piper's article in the *Archie Rev*, saying 'help against a schematic inhuman treatment of contemporary architectural problems is much needed'. That is why his retreat to 'Sharawaggi' and the principles of the Picturesque movement of the eighteenth century were so important and allowed to feature with such emphasis in his editorial. He hoped, rather than believed, that Sharawaggi, the distribution of these bare housing units in random attractive patterns, some vertical, some horizontal, among mature trees and irregularities of the land, would solve the monotony. He found Point Royal, the seventeen-storey block of flats by Arup Associates in Bracknell, Berkshire, 'very powerful', but 'not tower-like enough. It calls for four or five more of identical design. They could then create their own environment.' He believed that Nature would rescue humanity provided a bold course was followed. At what point should he have noticed that this was not happening and called a halt?

There is a case to be made for considering Pevsner as critically unsound, an aesthetic dualist with one side of his appreciative faculty attuned to enjoy ornament and decorative indulgence, the other side manic and obsessive in the belief that, though human nature had gone through no radical changes in the twentieth century, a machine age still had the right to demand machine solutions. Remember again that question he posed in June 1945, when a Labour government, of no very great artistic sophistication but of great social urgency, had just come to power at Westminster: how could a democratic society 'be brought round to the saving grace of a Bauhaus style without the application of force?' One answer lies in the persuasive writings of prestigious figures such as Pevsner. That is the responsibility which those early volumes of the *Buildings of England* have to bear.

The corollary, of course, is that Betjeman and Piper too must share a certain amount of blame for setting up such an ineffectual and ill-conceived counterforce in their *Murray's Guides*. They had had the advantage of striking first. *Buckinghamshire* came out in 1948, *Berkshire* in 1949, and that forlorn venture *Lancashire* in 1950. So much was good about them. Their joint authors had wit, an English cultural background, good intentions and subtle perceptions on their side. Their publisher gave them the pictorial back-up they required. Yet the series, which was to cover all England, ran into the sands after only three counties. What went wrong?

The answer lay in the format. A wonderfully potent and educative section of photographs with well-tuned captions was, in the first guide, *Buckinghamshire*, completely unrelated to a grudging gazetteer, printed without the relief of any illustration on ugly paper. Betjeman, over-occupied with hack journalism, must take the blame for this. Entries in the gazetteer were too few, too short and too dull. Pevsner's later *Buckinghamshire*, researched by Mark Girouard, was superior in almost every respect. Piper had to go through Betjeman's captions sharpening them up. For Chetwode church, for instance, it was Piper who, at the proofing stage, scribbled in a fierce, 'Opposite the old glass, in the north wall, is modern stained glass out of harmony and out of scale with everything else – an instance of twentieth century arrogance beside Victorian sensibility.' It took courage and self-confidence to make a point like that in 1948, years before the Victorian come-back.

It was not the gazetteer alone that was ill-conceived – the second, *Berkshire*, has a splendid gazetteer. The problem was more general. The *Murray's Guides* had none of the *Shell Guides'* popular immediacy. Their dust-jackets were dull and at 18 shillings a copy, when the last *Shells* and the earliest *Pevsners* had been priced at 3s 6d, they were too expensive. On the other hand, what was brilliant about them was the way in which they not only presented the historical progress and individuality of their respective counties but also effortlessly conveyed quite subtle stylistic perceptions. To look at their photographs was to be made to think, to differentiate and to discern.

It was the range as well as the quality of Piper's photographs that was so impressive. To take just a few examples, no one following his ruthless photography and cruel captions could ever again take Jeffry Wyatville's toy-fort additions to Windsor Castle seriously or rate highly the repetitious, unsatisfying nature of the Perpendicular Gothic in St George's Chapel. He evoked the yokel crudity of clunch as a stone for carving, conveyed by one shot of The Deanery (Deanery Garden) at Sonning the confident asymmetries of Lutyens. I recall having my own mind opened to the inventive possibilities of a style and a period I had always scorned, the Edwardian, just by Piper's photograph of a house at Pangbourne with his acid-sharp caption: 'It is one of a group called "The Seven Deadly Sins" by those who think decoration is immoral.' In one neat, short tilt he had run a spear of common sense not only through Pevsner but also through the entire dreary history of puritan simplicity in English art.

There was another, unforgettable photograph and caption of a very early nineteenth-century house, 72 High Street, Marlow, where, Piper urged persuasively,

> we find an extraordinarily complete realization of the ideals of modern architects of the 1919–39 period, saved from mere stark-ness by the delicate patterning of the slender glazing bars. Unfortunately, the Georgian Revivalists, instead of picking up the thread where it was dropped, go back fifty or a hundred years earlier, and produce boring, if well meant designs, or restorations like the Post Office on the other side of the High Street.

An entire essay on architecture has been compressed here into one potent paragraph, a rebuke to Modernists and neo-Georgians alike, a plea for a historical continuity lost by Victorian historicism. It was a point Morton Shand was forever trying to make, but he got lost in his examples. Pevsner, with what John Carter, a director of the publishers Scribner's, rudely described as 'his tortuous and Teutonic style', could never make points so convincingly, partly because his *Pevsners* deliberately divorced the image from the script. Even when he was anxious to defend his favourite style and make converts, as when he was writing on A. D. Connell's mould-breaking house of 1929–31, 'High and Over' at Amersham, all Pevsner could manage was:

> The bare concrete walls, the sharply cut-in horizontal windows, the meeting of unrelieved cubic shapes, the fully glazed staircase, all these are now familiar features – they were shockingly new in England then. The concrete water-tank on the highest point of the site is a shock still – a circular pole with a large circular cistern like a millstone high up. The plan of the house is a hexagonal centre and three radial wings, completely symmetrical, but varied in height so that no formality appears in the elevations. Only one wing runs up to full height, and this has a one-storeyed addition at its end; the other two have only one upper floor but roof canopies on this.

A house like that could have been made to sing in defiant prose. It was part of Pevsner's faith that we should build like this, but where was his liturgy? At the end of his account he admits, writing in 1960, that 'it still looks alien now. Why is that?', but he knows the answer. Conventional Voyseydom had returned, houses 'that never had any intention of hitting as hard as the Connell and Ward houses'. Exactly who or what did Nikolaus want to hit? With what forces did he think he was fighting?

Nothing illustrates the distance between the Betjeman aesthetic and Pevsnerian priorities better than the way in which the two men approached Uffington, home ground for both of them. John, who must have had his knuckles rapped sharply by Piper after his lame entries on Buckinghamshire, wrote twice

Pevsner's word count, storming in with uninhibited picture-postcard raptures of 'chalk-built cottages sheltering under great elms', 'a willow-bordered stream and footpaths', even informing the reader of the White Horse Hill's trick of 'looking large and near before rain and distant in hot weather'. An inability to be embarrassed was one of Betjeman's greatest strengths; it left him free to be natural with no need to strike detached poses.

After considering Uffington's associations with *Tom Brown's Schooldays* — Tom had attended the village school before being sent away to Rugby — he turned to a lengthy account of the White Horse, or dragon, carved in the hillside. Here his Edith Olivier instincts took over. Readers were given romantic snatches — a grassless patch of ground where the dragon's blood had fallen, the village mummers' play of St George, fertility rituals, old cheese-rolling rites — then he returned to the real world with mention of a 'primeval-looking wood', 'disused watercress beds' and a suggestion for a walk with fine views. That left the church, St Mary's, where he had been for a while a churchwarden. Here there is a problem. Betjeman not only gets the date of his own church wrong but also that of the building of Salisbury Cathedral, 1150 instead of 1250, and he makes the same mistake twice. Could it be a misprint? If not it is a worrying instance of John's often cavalier attitude towards scholarship. To put Uffington's exceptionally pure, wiry, Early English Gothic building slap in the middle of the Angevin Romanesque period is a howler from any guide writer. He is sound, but no more, on 'the deep precision of its mouldings and general excellence of proportion', 'a fairly harmless' (actually rather dreadful) restoration by G. E. Street in 1850 and the various monuments, pitch-pine benches and fragments of screen. But the church has one outstanding oddity and mystery, two unique side chapels, triangular-gabled with straight mullions to the windows. These Betjeman never even mentions and it is at points like these that Pevsner races ahead.

His Uffington is a no-nonsense affair, the usual graceless staccato of verbless sentences, headings and hard facts. Half of it, the first half, is devoted to St Mary's with the architectural historian's arcane vocabulary at full stretch: 'Outer and inner doors have mature stiff-leaf capitals', 'a three-light Dec window with reticulated tracery', 'the rib profile not one of the current ones'. If that rib profile wasn't current, what was it? He goes on. 'The capitals of the shafts are polygonal, as though they were Perp. But they are not.' Caught you there, you ignorant tourist! And the crossing arches 'present something odd once more, the abaci with concave hollows as if they were Perp'. A puzzled visitor retires to consult the glossary at the back. This is Pevsner on Perp, at his best and at his worst. He dearly loved a problem and Uffington presented about fifteen, a rich harvest. Not for him an idle (though very shrewd) speculation that a Salisbury-trained mason had designed the church; he could hardly trail after Betjeman. But he solved the problem of the triangular-gabled side chapels by consulting the vicar. They were work of 1678, hence their un-Gothicity. The churchwardens' accounts of 1677–9 recorded, 'Payd to John Deane for ye end wall of ye Church, pulling it downe & setting it up £25.0.0.' This is something which a much later churchwarden should have had the scholarly curiosity to have found out for himself.

Pevsner gave the White Horse an admirable literary historical treatment with interesting reactions to it by Celia Fiennes – 'perfect proportions' – Francis Wise and Robert Dodsley. He also corrected Betjeman's assertion that the Cerne Giant was a proven prehistoric hill figure. Not for Pevsner the merry cheese-rolling ceremonies or an antiquary's note on the 'scouring of the horse'; for him 'the grooming is done by the Ministry of Public Buildings and Works'. Sometimes it is tempting to think that Nikolaus deliberately lived up to the public image of a prim, prosy Pevsner. John Newman has discovered three instances of Pevsner humour in the forty-six volumes; this might go down as the fourth.

Helpful, fact-packed accounts of three British or Romano-British earthworks in the parish rounded off Pevsner's Uffington: there were no viewpoints, not a single cottage and no

Tom Brown references, but a thoroughly scholarly résumé in broken prose, half of it demanding the familiarity with a special vocabulary that *Pevsner*-users quickly acquire. It teaches English history in its way but not in an evocative, Kiplingesque way: mysteries are there to be solved not set up.

By 1951, when the first three *Pevsners* came out, Murray's had given up on their *Guides*. Betjeman and Piper, who had been retracing their 1939 steps to bring out a Shropshire guide at last, had turned back to Shell who were now, with the petrol flowing again, ready to restart their series with Faber and Faber as the publishers. The Shell *Shropshire*, so brilliant and idiosyncratic, so cruelly delayed, came out in the same year, 1951. The race was now running level. It is often forgotten in all the celebrations over forty-six *Pevsners* that there were over thirty *Shell Guides*, with wonderfully individual new counties by Henry Thorold, the squire, priest and antiquary: *Staffordshire*, *Durham* and *Derbyshire*; then *Lancashire* with Jack Yeats; Norman Scarfe's *Suffolk*, *Essex* and *Cambridgeshire*; and James Lees-Milne's *Worcestershire*. Betjeman hailed this last as 'awfully good and the best of the series to date', a remark which he seems to have made, in his usual kindly way, to everyone in his stable of authors. Then there were those dangerously dark and dank, almost Stone Age *Shell Guides* by Vyvyan Rees: *South West Wales*, *Mid Western Wales* and *Mid Eastern Wales*, all hewn from the rock of a foreign country. Piper himself brought out, with J. H. Cheetham, a new *Wiltshire*, Michael Pitt-Rivers a new *Dorset*. The *Shells* were as virile as the *Pevsners* in renewing themselves, but they never caught the nation's imagination as they did not aim to be entirely inclusive or drily factual.

Shells and *Pevsners* were not, however, exactly comparable. The *Shells* were always true guide-books, designed to lure readers to a county, to make explorations and, but only incidentally, to make them grow wisely aware. If one on the appropriate local county were a required text for school-leavers in every secondary school in the country, studied, enjoyed, explored and, by some practical means, examined, the whole nation would be more at ease with where it lives. The *Pevsners* on the other hand were conceived as reference books to which one could turn, after making a discovery, for more information. As such they grew better and better, as Pevsner always intended they should. He described, generously but accurately, John Newman's two *Pevsners* on Kent as the best in the series. That was true in 1969 when the two were published. Now Bridget Cherry and Nikolaus Pevsner's *London 2: South* of 1983 and Edward Hubbard's *Clwyd* of 1986 rate even higher. The former takes an exceptionally complex area and never loses a light appreciative touch despite a blizzard of exact information; the latter evokes the dark decay of ruined industry and a racial intermix of opposed cultures with a rare empathy for two nations in a border country. But try struggling up that steep street of architectural intensity that leads from the side of Greenwich Palace to Blackheath with Bridget Cherry's heavyweight in your hand and its limitations as a guide become pressingly obvious.

Nikolaus, for all his twelve-mile walks (although John Harris in his *No Voice from the Hall* maintains that he 'was not one for hiking' and certainly 'not one for climbing through windows'), was not a natural guide-book writer. He can only have urged his *Buildings of England* upon Allen Lane as 'guides' to make them sound like popular money-spinners. The editions of 20,000 and 30,000 that Lane risked in his first enthusiasm sold very slowly. Works of reference were always Pevsner's aim and he intended to learn himself as he wrote them, but the best volumes were written by other scholars: John Newman, Bridget Cherry, John Harris, Ian Nairn, Edward Hubbard. The entire series would have been better if Pevsner had been more ready to step back and let the natives take over. His publishers were losing £3,000 on each slim paperback volume in the early 1950s and the series would have come to the same end as the *Murray's Guides* if the Leverhulme Trust and various other benefactors had not stepped in with subsidies.

A letter from Pevsner to Allen Lane of 15 May 1967 reveals that he had chosen John Newman to be his editorial heir if he died before the English series was complete. In the event Nikolaus lived to see England rounded off by *Staffordshire* in 1974, Scotland and Wales begun, and the splendidly superior, even heavier second editions come rumbling out. So Newman can hardly be considered an impartial judge, for he was involved in their creation. Nevertheless, if *Pevsners* need an advocate, as sometimes they do, Newman's defence of them deserves a précis.

In brief, he claims that their author was often humorous but could be moved by beauty. Sometimes he was awed, occasionally disgusted by a building. He could be responsive to the personality of a builder or a patron, though more often he homed in on structural histories. Newman allowed that he could be biased in favour of buildings from transitional stylistic periods, was more interested in the medieval than the classical, was bored by Palladianism, obsessive to a degree over spatial effects as opposed to linear or decorative ones, was devoted to landscape gardens, ultimately disillusioned over tower-blocks, pro-William Morris and pro-Decorated (but not Perpendicular) Gothic and, finally, enjoyed the advantage of being a foreigner, a point which can be interpreted in more ways than one. Most of Newman's claims will stand scrutiny. A devil's advocate could, however, put a good case for the prosecution.

Because of their format the *Pevsners* never work practically as guides, rarely inducing the reader to visit a particular area. Starting off as drab, little brown paperbacks they quickly became unwieldy and expensive books of reference for the already converted. Their photographs are mostly mug-shots, badly printed and clumped together in the middle of the text with wilfully uninspiring captions. Unlike the illustrations in a *Shell Guide* they lend no helping hand to the text and their actual provision is ungenerous. An average *Pevsner* entry, 90 per cent of the total, is dry as dust, visually weak and, as a deliberate policy, perversely written to avoid any opening comment of admiration, praise or denigration which could set the mood. Far too many words are spent on churches, particularly churches with any problems of construction. Lists of church plate are a waste of time as it can never be inspected. With his political mistrust of England's class system and dislike of the aristocracy, Pevsner underplays the great country houses, misses out entirely many fine lesser houses and, if he gives an account of them, over-stresses the architect at the expense of the patron and owner. It was not his fault that he began publishing before the invaluable scholarship of Howard Colvin, in his great *Biographical Dictionary of British Architects*, came out in 1954, and before John Summerson's seminal *Architecture in Britain* of 1953. Even so, he is weak on source material because he was a foreigner and naturally under-informed on British authorities. After his first sensible *Middlesex*, which even marks parish boundaries, the maps in subsequent *Pevsners* were grossly inadequate; and the introductory essays on geology, history and stylistic development lacked illustrations and were too long and isolated from the gazetteers.

There is much to be said for and against, but after that blast of criticism, it needs to be stressed that the *Pevsners* only attract strong feelings because they are generally acknowledged as a potent resource of national reference. Nevertheless they were and are used not only by middle-class tourists and architectural enthusiasts, but also by planners and predatory architects looking for prestigious support in schemes of demolition and profitable rebuilding. In his lifetime Sir Nikolaus Pevsner became a name to conjure with, sometimes for the weaving of very black spells. Even so, Betjeman might seem to have been uncharacteristically intransigent when, in a letter of 18 July 1953, Alec Clifton-Taylor asked to be allowed to review a *Pevsner* favourably in *Time and Tide*. 'We cannot continue to praise Pevsner,' John replied, 'the guides . . . are neither complete as a catalogue nor distinctive as a personal approach.' He believed that Pevsner had relied for the most part on 'a series of *studentium* who have gone around getting things out of directories and sometimes using their own eyes, but not, I suspect, often.'

There was real anger here. Richard Ingrams later commented on 'the strange and one-sided feud' which Betjeman had conducted against 'the Herr Doktor Professor'. There was, Ingrams believed, 'nothing personal in it. It was just that Betjeman thought of that inventory approach to churches as a kind of blasphemy which it was his duty to attack.' Ingrams was wrong. The feud was neither 'strange' nor was it 'one-sided'. He was, however, correct in believing that Pevsner's approach to churches had been responsible for the bitterness. Prior to 1952 the mildly xenophobic Betjeman had never warmed to Pevsner's writing nor to his presence on the English architectural scene, but when open warfare broke out between the two men in that year it was, surprisingly, Nikolaus not John who fired the first shot, a raking, provocative and deliberately hurtful broadside.

Ninian Comper may or may not have been the most impressive British church architect of the twentieth century, but he was certainly the most gloriously high camp. Predictably Betjeman treasured him, entertained him in expensive restaurants and dined at The Priory, Comper's Regency Gothic villa in Upper Norwood. As a living and still highly active Victorian architect and fellow Anglo-Catholic, Comper was a natural hero for Betjeman. In 1950 he had secured a knighthood for the 86-year-old gentleman and he continued to write up his church interiors in breathless technicoloured prose. On Aberdeen Cathedral's east end for instance:

> White plaster vaulting diminishes away in perspective adorned with baroque gold and coloured shields. And there, far at the east end, is a great baldachin over the altar in burnished gold with a spire like that on King's College. And beyond the gold of the baldachin, intensely gold in this blazing whiteness, you see the deep blue tints, the green and the red of Comper's large east window.

Contemptuously aware of this Comper-olatry, Pevsner used his 1952 *London: Volume 2* to attack Comper's St Cyprian, Marylebone, in a judicious yet woundingly dismissive appraisal:

If there must be medieval imitations in the c20 it is here unques-
tionably done with joy and care. Beyond that appreciation can
hardly go. There is no reason for the excesses of praise lavished on
Comper's church furnishings by those who confound aesthetic with
religious emotions.

St Cyprian's, as he must have known, was Betjeman's favourite London Comper, a church which he brought Modernists like
de Cronin Hastings and J. M. Richards to see and admire. From
that time onwards the gloves were off. Writing to James Lees-
Milne in March 1952 Betjeman was fuming about these 'new
refugee "scholars"'. Then in a letter of 31 October to Morton
Shand he described Thomas Howarth's new book on
Mackintosh as 'a singularly ugly book, and a typical "thesis". I
think Granny [Pevsner] appears on every page.' It was precisely
'the new kind of art history which kills architecture'. In the following year in a *Times Literary Supplement* review (3 July
1953) of the latest *Pevsner* on County Durham he wrote,
anonymously, a savage but considered attack on Pevsner's scholarship and the whole concept of his guides.

First he ridiculed his working methods, describing how
Pevsner depended 'much on information provided by others
and even his reading had to be done by proxy. After a hectic
period of personal visits the material was hurriedly put
together.' Next he found 'slips and mistakes on almost every
page', so that 'there comes a point when these militate against
the usefulness of the book'. He claimed that Pevsner's 'account
of the conversion of the North will make the historian wince
from time to time'. Then came a crushing, point-by-point enu-
meration of Pevsner's 'sins of omission and commission', chiefly
Saxon but also prehistoric, seventeenth- and eighteenth-
century, a 500-word exposure of a foreigner's pitiful ignorance
of an English county. John was usually completely at sea on
matters Anglo-Saxon, but here his Saxon scholarship was
deadly in its accuracy. Either he had spent days researching the
review or he had taken the informed advice of a local Durham

historian. On dating, stonework, vaulting and even Saxon sun-dials he found Pevsner's book riddled with inaccuracies, finally doubting 'whether any useful purpose had been served by this high-pressure, stream-lined method of producing a guide book . . . the careless and worse than careless mistakes scattered throughout the book will form a source of annoyance to those who know their Durham County well, and a source of confu-sion to those who do not'.

Alec Clifton-Taylor had been, from his student days, a friend and admirer of Pevsner and he was outraged. His request to be allowed to publish a defence in *Time and Tide*, a weekly review where John was poetry editor and literary adviser, was rejected. Meanwhile Pevsner was allowed a letter of reply in the 24 July issue of the *TLS*. This was an incoherent, apologetic disaster. He admitted that most of the reviewer's criticisms on matters of Saxon accuracy were correctly aimed and humbly thanked his anonymous persecutor for information on seventeenth-century staircases 'which I had indeed not seen nor read about'. More damagingly, it was evident from the unedited writing that Pevsner was still not fluent in English. Two of his sentences lacked any verb, 'apodictic' was used unidiomatically and the general tone was one of plaintive, repetitive spluttering. Silence would have been much wiser. He had deliberately hurt Betjeman in that vulnerable area where religious enthusiasms and aesthetic judgements interact. Now he himself had been ridiculed as an outsider whose scholarship was inadequate in an English context. In future he would keep a tactful, even nervous, distance where matters concerning Betjeman and controversy were involved.

It had been an episode out of character. For someone who wrote so many millions of words, chiefly on architecture, Pevsner was usually extraordinarily reserved in his judgements. That is why, in an earlier chapter dealing with his *Pioneers of the Modern Movement*, I have paid so much attention to his comments on painters. Writing on artists like Renoir, Toorop and Cézanne, Pevsner was prepared to reveal far more of his own emotional reactions than he was over architects. Similarly with his first volume, *Middlesex*, he was on home ground and much less guarded than he was to become later, so it repays a close scrutiny. The slim 1951 paperback was written in the austere 1946–7 period and, perhaps out of a sense of reverent respect for the first steps of the master, it has never been followed up by a second edition but has remained lost in subsequent reorganizations, like the county of Middlesex itself.

If any single entry sums up the man it is an eight-line account of all that Alperton, a suburb in Acton parish, near the Surrey border, offered:

> L. T. STATION by *Charles Holden*, 1933. One of that excellent set of designs produced in 1932 and 1933 which did so much to establish the modern idiom in Britain. Modest, functional, yet not without elegance. Comparisons with such other Piccadilly Line stations as Sudbury Town, Sudbury Hill, Oakwood will repay; the same motifs are every time subtly modified (the right mixture of standardization and variation).

How Nikolaus loved Frank Pick! He had been the prime mover of London Transport for years, dispensing design patronage like a second Medici, his modest buildings 'not without elegance', combining 'standardization and variation'. Clean, functional, ever-so-slightly dull, these stations were what Pevsner meant by the architecture of the twentieth century. But if these were the ideal stations for suburbia what, in Pevsner's opinion, were the ideal suburban houses? Flats, factories and offices were easily thrown up in 'the modern idiom', but when it came to housing the millions Pevsner had been mildly contemptuous of the style of successful 'factory' estates like Port Sunlight and Bournville. So in *Middlesex* it would be useful to try and pin him down on this one issue that really matters socially.

An aesthetic trap had been set for him as long ago as 1875 when Jonathan Carr chose Richard Norman Shaw, the cosiest and most readily acceptable of Victorian architects, to design the houses of Bedford Park. This, England's first planned garden suburb, is also in Acton parish but at a wide social remove from Alperton. It still survives substantially unchanged as pure Merchant-Ivory territory, leafy, graciously middle, even upper-middle class. Its vaguely Dutch-style brick houses have those touches of individual charm – bay windows, demure porches, inset brickwork – which intelligent people usually require if they have the money to pay for them. So in that sense it is Port Sunlight a few steps up the class ladder and a perfect demonstration, which Le Corbusier naturally chose to ignore, of precisely the kind of *machine à habiter* that men and women really want: one that satisfies vanity, the imagination and individuality.

Bedford Park presented a problem for Pevsner and one which he evaded quite skilfully. After noting, with cool precision, 'Dutch gables and tile-hung gables, much use of decorative tiles, white window casements, white little oriels, cosy porches, etc.', he took refuge behind other writers' opinions instead of delivering his own. There was William Morris's 'quaint and pretty architecture', and the *St James's Gazette* of 1881's mocking thrust: Bedford Park 'where men may lead a chaste correct Aesthetical existence'. He did not bring in Gilbert and Sullivan's 'greenery yallery, Grosvenor Gallery, je ne sais quoi young man', though he might well have done. Instead he ended disdainfully with 'the arty character of the early population of Bedford Park is familiar from G. K. Chesterton's *The Man who was Thursday*' and rounded off the entry with No. 14 South Parade, Voysey's tower-house for Mrs Forster, 'designed evidently in conscious opposition to the red-brick cosiness of the suburb'. This critical reserve is typical of Pevsner's writing, and it enabled him deliberately and ungenerously to avoid any commendation of an entirely successful design solution. Here, and with his very different reaction to Hampstead Garden Suburb, it is possible to understand, though not to sympathize with, the distortion central to Pevsner's architectural judgement. In theory he was committed to the socialist ideals and design solutions of the Bauhaus; in real life middle-class England had seduced him and won him over to the layout and aesthetics of Hampstead Garden Suburb.

To describe this celebrated housing development as a very superior council-house estate gives the wrong social, though not entirely the wrong visual, impression of the place. As you walk its little hedge-bound short cuts, quiet closes, unrectangular crossings and apparently traffic-less streets, just the faintest air of council planning and nanny-knows-best direction hangs over it. Dame Henrietta Barnett set up a trust to build the Garden Suburb in 1906. It was to provide homes ranging across the class barriers, with no pubs for demon drink and with commerce kept at a distance, so it is easy to see why Pevsner not only approved of its ideals but also determined, when he settled down to be British, to live as near to it in 1935 as he could afford and to hail it, in his first ever *Pevsner* guide, as 'The aesthetically most satisfactory and socially most successful of all c20 garden suburbs'. That was before giving it a five-page spread, the kind of treatment usually reserved for Romsey Abbey or Blenheim Palace. It is the happiest possible proof that he had a heart after all. He even mentioned several 'neo-William-and-Mary-houses' in his own Wildwood Road, where the Quaker friends with whom he had been staying had found him a house at a modest rent in which he was to live for the rest of his life. But does this sentimental, likeable weakness reveal a basic hypocrisy in his stylistic stance? He begins, for instance, by claiming social success for the Hampstead experiment, with its mixed accommodation, suited to a wide class range, but then admits that over the last few years it has become entirely middle-class in its residents, has no bus service, too few shops and a social centre – Lutyens's St Jude, the Free Church and the Institute – which is dead because the controlling trust forbids cinemas, pubs and cafés.

His most serious and revealing admission has to do with the style of the houses, which are by Lutyens, Raymond Unwin and Barry Parker, Baillie-Scott and others. While praising unreservedly the overt historicism of Lutyens's contributions, 'a fine restrained late c17 formality, in grey brick with red-brick dressing', he remarks complacently that most of the houses are

> in a free and comfortable neo-Tudor brick architecture which has indeed stood the test of forty years splendidly. The brick-work is sensitive throughout, of uneven surface and varying in colour from grey to dark purple-reds. The roofs are usually steep-pitched and with many gables.

Everything, in fact, apart from Lutyens's superior neo-Georgian, is sub-Voysey. Pevsner, like Betjeman, had always admired Voysey though he was never able convincingly to relate Voysey's neo-Tudor to the Modern Movement. He always realized, in a secretive inner Nikolaus, that Voysey's style worked and that Voysey's was likely to be the future of English housing. Here in Hampstead was the living proof of it, so why should he have persisted in looking further, to an International Modernism of the New Century? It is very hard to see him as anything but a resounding hypocrite on this one point, consigning the 'artisan classes' to domestic experiments which were most unlikely to work while he lived contentedly in a middle-class, wholly traditional, ghetto.

There is another instance of his perverse illogicality in a neighbouring county, Buckinghamshire, and in a national monument, Eton College. When Betjeman wrote up Eton town and the College for that *Murray's Guide* of 1948 he confined himself to a conventional note on the chapel: 'Soaring proportions, delicate precision of shafted stonework and an overwhelming effect of size', which is adequate writing but no more. When Pevsner arrived there for his 1960 *Buckinghamshire* (research assistant Mark Girouard, fresh from the Courtauld Institute), the Fellows of Eton had very recently employed one of Pevsner's favourite architects, Sir William Holford, to give their chapel a new vault, and Pevsner was as near to horror as he ever allowed himself to become. He had greatly admired Holford's cold, Modernist blocks for the new precincts of St Paul's Cathedral (Betjeman had decried them as characterless and built at the wrong height) but now, here at Eton, Pevsner's hero had resorted to a traditional fan vault, and a fake fan vault at that, one of 'light-weight concrete, stone-faced and set in T-section steel framing'. 'Architects on the Continent,' Pevsner complained, 'faced with buildings damaged in the Second World War, have shown that a radical juxtaposition of old and new can come off', but now Holford had sold out to the traditionalists.

This is a central issue in the Pevsner debate. He had, it will be recalled, insisted that a Modernist insertion between two nineteenth-century brownstone houses in New York was 'highly successful'. All over Britain developers were getting away with stylistic murder on the strength of this Pevsner premise: that a cheap modern block accorded excitingly if it was slammed in between two older buildings. Any effort to match the work on either side would have been expensive, with decorative detail from highly paid craftsmen, so if profits were to be kept high this myth of the adaptability of the modern style had to be projected, and everywhere, in all the journals and broadsheets, hack writers went along with the legend, following the lead of Pevsner. In Communist states like Poland and Russia royal palaces would be rebuilt from the rubble and entire quarters of cities like Vilnius restored in their original style, but in capitalist Britain the cheap way out was taken. Holford's St Paul's precinct is the perfect example, and Pevsner, blinkered by an ideal, nodded approval.

Here, in his entry on Eton's chapel, the tortuous processes of his mind and his impracticality can be followed. What was his ideal solution?

> Basil Spence's vault for his cathedral at Coventry is designed to be of the c20 yet not out of sympathy with the Gothic past. Admittedly, a vault like that projected for Coventry would not have done for Eton. What should it then have looked like? The critic is in the enviable position of not having to give an answer.

And to that astonishing evasion he added an analytical dishonesty by trying to prove that a fan vault might not have been the original builder's intention. He noted the outside buttresses and the five shafts at the springing of each bay which 'could point to a fan vault', but still insisted, completely unconvincingly for such an aisle-less chapel, that it could have been a lierne vault, which was sheer niggling pedantry.

And yet, after all that gratuitous carping, his account of the College as a whole is masterly, infinitely superior to Betjeman's. John lost himself as usual in reverent whimsy about 'a lamp post like the "Burning Bush", opposite the College, and that delightful early pillar box, fluted Doric style in the High Street'. Pevsner followed the College's architectural history through lucidly from Henry VI to Holford and still had space for the telling details of the wall paintings 'executed *c.* 1479–88 and paid for to at least two painters, one *Gilbert*, the other *William Baker*'. Against vivid Pevsner snatches like 'Amoras selling his wife to the devil', and 'the man who threw a stone at an image of the Virgin and fell down dead when he saw blood gush forth from a child's body', Betjeman can only offer 'Flemish style wall paintings, (*c.* 1480)'. That is one reason why the *Pevsners* succeeded: they tell so much, the scholarship is usually so satisfying. Betjeman's accounts are often so very thin; his perceptions were sound but academically he was inadequate or uninterested. In a rare personal comment on his rival, Nikolaus described Betjeman's 'Introduction' to Collins's *Guide to English Parish Churches* as 'superb, but the gazetteer is done in an extraordinarily uneven way. Wherever you have a paragraph of John Betjeman's own writing it is worth reading.'

Sometimes, as at East Claydon in the same county, Betjeman can carry it off. This is Pevsner's entry on the White House in that parish:

> NW of the church. This has a porch with a Victorian date 1662. It looks rather earlier. The entrance still has a four-centred head. Flanking pilasters. Front garden with c18 brick wall.

Compare that with Betjeman's shameless violin strings of evocative nostalgia:

a fragment of a large house behind its yew hedges and wall of seventeenth century red brick is an unspoilt example of the kind of houses Englishmen built themselves in the age when Shakespeare wrote *The Tempest* and Milton *Il Penseroso*. A hundred years ago it was reputed to possess a ghost; it is probably still haunted by the happy spirits of people who lived in it and loved it.

He was still playing the 'How to Catch a Pixie' game and Edith Olivier must have turned in her grave at the plagiarism of her method. 'Beat that, Pevsner!' he might have said, but Pevsner would have scorned to try. In the same county there was a Modern-style Rank Laboratory, a work by the master himself, Gropius, with assistance from Maxwell Fry, 1936. Pevsner refused to show any hint of excitement or even pleasure:

Long front with parts of various heights, the l. one with long balconies of corrugated iron on two floors. Then a raised bit and a r. part with windows on three storeys. Doorway with canopy on thin shafts, a motif often repeated since. The building is relatively unknown.

No violin strings sobbing here; was he, perhaps, just a shade disappointed to see theory realized in actuality? He could, on occasion, strike muted lyrical notes, as in Ludford, Shropshire: 'a village of great charm, leafy below Whitcliffe'; or Dropmore House in Buckinghamshire: 'Long, white and delightfully unassuming . . . in a veritable orgy of trellis, including Greek Doric temple fronts with single and coupled columns. In the centre of these long pergolas an AVIARY of iron and green Chinese pottery panels', though in this instance the house itself was probably encouraging him to write well. Curiously, Betjeman only mentions the arboretum.

Quite why Pevsner, who as Newman says preferred the medieval to the classical, could rarely manage even a hint of rapture for the churches that fascinated him, is obscure. Did their function – of psalms, chanting, ritual, music and the Godhead – disturb him, or did he lack a seeing eye? At

Claverley in Shropshire, a large church with 'spatial variety', the quality he most enjoyed, he had to admit, 'It is not easy to visualise the church as it was *c.* 1200. It must have been of remarkably ambitious dimensions, with the nave as wide as now, and a S tower, and a N aisle.' He says he could not visualize it, yet Claverley has a glorious procession of wall paintings of about 1200, with horses, horsemen, trees and presiding angels, a rough and ready Norman-English anticipation of a Guilio Romano room in the Palazzo del Te at Mantua, and still Pevsner says he cannot visualize what it was like. He tucks the paintings away under 'FURNISHINGS' but gives a fair photograph of them, a fifty-foot concentration of the imagination of the Middle Ages.

Again and again when a photograph in a *Pevsner* is intriguing and the reader turns to the relevant entry it refuses to blow the trumpet of enthusiastic prose. Brixworth church in Northamptonshire is a large, mysterious building of the seventh century, unique in England. Here, with extreme antiquity and great structural complexities to unravel, Pevsner will surely unbend. But, no, he plays the same game that he played at Bedford Park; he hides behind another man's quotation and opens his admirably clear analysis with: 'ALL SAINTS. "Perhaps the most imposing architectural memorial of the seventh century surviving north of the Alps" (Clapham)', then goes on cautiously to undercut even that with: 'That the building belongs essentially to the c7 is convincing though not conclusively provable.'

Fortunately there were still alternative voices. They may have been overtaken but the *Shell Guides* were still being published, as individual and enticing as ever. Their *Northamptonshire* came out in 1968 and in it Lady Juliet Smith opened her account of Brixworth with:

> The famous church at Brixworth dates from that strange twilight age when Roman Britain was slowly crumbling into ruin. The later Saxons were to take melancholy pleasure in musing on the past of the great empty halls and palaces.

Before she took on that *Shell Guide*, Juliet Smith had been lectured by John in one of his last editorial functions before he resigned in 1967 with his task, if not complete, then at least half done, and half done brilliantly. 'It is no good trying to write a comprehensive, impersonal catalogue,' he told her. 'That is being done already in Pevsner's *Buildings of England*, and does not tell you what the place is really like . . . it is the eye and the heart that are the surest guides.' Writing earlier to thank James Lees-Milne for his *Worcestershire* guide he congratulated him because 'There is so much affection and delicious grumpiness in it.' Lees-Milne had just, in his *Shell Guide*, ranked the mayor and councillors of Worcester alongside the Vikings and Oliver Cromwell for the way in which they had vandalized the heart of their own city by an inner ring road. 'Every sentence', Betjeman went on, 'shows eye, heart and brain and stands for a personal visit'; and in April 1966 he told Piper jubilantly and competitively, 'We have got Pevsner on the run.' That was wishful thinking. The *Pevsners* were becoming a national institution and an unstoppable wave of scholarship; Pevsner was already, to use a half-admiring, half-mocking phrase from a comic poem by Peter Clarke, 'Der Great Categorist'. But if Nikolaus was not running, then at least, and at long last, the developers were, and it was in a *Shell* not a *Pevsner* that Lees-Milne was able to pour ridicule on a complacent city corporation. The nation had a conscience with a heart as well as a recorder with eye and brain. In the great conservation battles of the coming years it would need both.

CHAPTER SEVEN

'How to Get On in Society'

It was in the 1950s that Betjeman and Pevsner both became, independently of their guide-books, media celebrities – Pevsner first, through his 1955 Reith Lectures on 'The Englishness of English Art', Betjeman next, through the sensational success of his *Collected Poems* of 1958, which sold better than any poetry had since Lord Byron's *Childe Harold* in 1812. To celebrate such a remarkable double for his firm, Jock Murray had three copies of the poems bound in red velvet at a cost of £30 apiece. One was presented to the Queen, the second went to Betjeman and the third Murray kept for himself. The guide-books alone would eventually have brought Pevsner and Betjeman modest fame, but 'The Englishness' and the *Collected Poems* made them instantly recognizable names. From that time onwards they would be natural Establishment figures on committees, commissions and trusts: Betjeman would be the driving force in English conservation, Pevsner the solemn seal upon conservation enterprises, the authoritative voice and the natural chairman, probably to his own wry amusement, of bodies concerned with the preservation of the past when he was overtly far more enthusiastic about the future.

Before their apotheosis both had received the accolade of

portrayal in comic verse. John Lloyd pirated *The Pirates of Penzance* for his appreciative friend John:

> I am the very model of a perfect Betjemanian
> I know all the London churches, from R C to Sandemanian,
> I know that Neo-Gothick is the only truly cultural
> And my appetite for Butterfield is positively vultural.
> I've a suitable derision for folk-weave and for pottery
> And a corresponding passion both for Streetery and Scottery.

Peter Clarke of *The Times* wrote a wickedly xenophobic poem, three verses of which are quite enough, on the 'Herr Professor-Doktor'. It ran:

> From heart of Mittel Europe
>   I make der little trip
> to show those Englische dummkopfs
>   some echtdeutsch Scholarship.
> Viel Sehenswurdigkeiten
>   by others have been missed
> but now comes to enlighten
>   der Great Categorist.
>
> Der Georgian und Viktorien
>   ist 'so wie so' "getan"
> bei Herr Professor Richardtson
>   und Dichter Betjemann.
> While oders gifs you Stevenage
>   Stonehenge und Gilbert Scott
> Von Pleiocene to C19
>   *I* gifs der blooming lot!
>
> All rest shall be resisted
>   till every stone und brick
> is finally gelisted
>   by Herr Professor N–k.
> Mit broadcast, book und Lektur
>   roll in der L. S. D.
> Der Britisch Architektur –
>   Ach, dat's der game for me!

Pevsner had preceded his Reith 'Lektur' series with an illustrated guide and a résumé of its most telling points, then followed the series up with an expanded and annotated book
version, even more fully illustrated, of the lectures themselves,
published by the Architectural Press and dedicated to Hubert de
Cronin Hastings – all in all a timely and cleverly judged enter-
prise. The English, like most nations, will take a few sharp criticisms provided they are wrapped up in plausible flattery, and
the whole idea of an artistic unity stretching back to the Anglo-
Saxons and reaching forward to Pevsner's preferred version of
the present day was, and indeed still is, intriguing. Architecture,
painting, sculpture and literature were all yoked together and
described with the detachment of a friendly German. It almost
goes without saying that the last lecture was intended to persuade Pevsner's million or so middle-class and influential listeners that England had, to date, culpably missed out on the
Modern Movement and the sooner they caught up with the new
style and reshaped their bomb-damaged cities with tower-
blocks arranged according to the Picturesque dictates of
Uvedale Price and fellow eighteenth-century enthusiasts, the
better.

Pevsner held, in effect, a Claude glass to English history,
reducing it to an intelligible perspective, stimulating his listeners and readers to assessments and comparisons, an amusing and
valuable intellectual exercise, valuable, that is, if Pevsner's own
judgements were taken merely as a starting-point. It was unfortunate that in his foreword Pevsner had to make exactly the
same ingenuous confession of apparent plagiarism as he had
made in the introduction to his *Pioneers*, nearly twenty years
earlier. In that he had claimed that it was only as he was
finishing the book that he discovered Philip Morton Shand had
been covering the same ground and had come to the same conclusions in the *Architectural Review*. Now he had discovered
that an Austrian, Professor Dagobert Frey, had published in
1942 *Englisches Wesen in der bildenen Kunst* (*The English
Character as Reflected in English Art*). By a striking coincidence,

Pevsner admitted, Professor Frey 'confirmed often to an amazing and almost embarrassing degree my views, the criteria I had worked out, even the examples I had chosen to illustrate them'.

Having put this 'almost' embarrassment behind him, Pevsner covered himself against any future accusations of inconsistency by stating that Englishness was both rational and irrational, and that there was 'a need for considering national character in contraries or polarities'. With this absolute freedom to claim any aspect of art as typically English he launched into a series of stimulating and perceptive generalizations, the most memorable and provable being that English fondness for repeating at length a single panelled motif without variation. This, at a stroke, justified Pevsner's low opinion of Perpendicular Gothic and Palladian architecture, for in neither style was the designer required to exercise much creative invention. He seems not to have realized, however, that if he had pursued that view a little further it would have undercut most applications of the principles of his treasured Modern Movement.

His lectures revealed how few periods of English architecture, and only brief ones at that, received Nikolaus's unreserved approval. There was the High Gothic, provided it offered subtle spatial qualities, as in the choir of Bristol Cathedral, the east end of Wells and the crossing of Ely, though not much else. He favoured some of John Vanbrugh's semi-Baroque palaces before the second Palladian revival made buildings predictable, and he admired Victorian feats of engineering. But at that point, though he was too polite to stress the fact, he came to a full stop. He was absolutely right to expose the insularity of English values in art and the ignorance of most self-satisfied English experts on continental equivalents within their field of specialism. And the bold range of his lectures – needlework, illuminated manuscripts, painting, sculpture and literature, though, curiously, not music – made them potent. They suggested an intellectual game that anyone with any claim to visual awareness could play with profit.

Let us suggest the ten greatest buildings or building complexes in Britain of any period. All of them must be strong enough candidates to rank unchallenged among the hundred greatest in Western Europe. Such a game can have sobering consequences. Interiors and exteriors must both satisfy, so how can Robert Adam's Syon House or Vanbrugh's Blenheim Palace qualify? One has a drab exterior, the other not a single great room within. Five cathedrals should romp home on anyone's list: Canterbury, Lincoln, Ely ... but then, are there five? Even with cathedrals, there comes a hesitation. Can Wells be included with that dwarfish nave and the owl eyes of the strainer arches peering down on it? What about heavily indigestible Winchester, or Exeter, rich and flowing but so low and unaspiring? York Minster might just get by on the excellence of its chapter-house as well as its glass. The chapel at King's College, Cambridge, is a possible, but being Perpendicular it is obsessively repetitious in its motifs.

So even the great churches make a shaky team. Allow five of them to stand alongside Burgos, Batalha, Chartres, Bourges, St Mark's and the other continental standard-setters, and the next five are even harder to conjure up. The Palace of Westminster goes forward, being stunning both inside and out. Hampton Court might scrape through on a combination ticket of Tudor and Wren, but this is debatable; is either sector really first-rate? Mackintosh's Hill House, Helensburgh, to show we are not always impressed by mere size, earns a place on its literally sublime domestic beauty; and, to irritate the Italians, Colen Campbell's Mereworth Castle in Kent might be slipped in since it is superior in its exteriors and its interiors to Palladio's Villa Rotunda, though sited less flatteringly.

Overall the ten which might stand up to the continental ninety do not come easily and that is why Pevsner's aloof viewpoint was so healthy. But with the mention of health, some reservations are required. Thinking back to the 1950s it is remarkable that Pevsner was allowed to get away with so much nonsense in his lectures. He made some absurd racist generalizations, such as that the English were a taciturn nation, speaking in low voices with 'a muffled sound'. Those 'bafflingly elongated statues on the west front of Wells' (are they so baffling if the portals of Chartres are recalled?) were 'long, lean, thin-faced and sparing in their movements – unmistakably types you see about in town and country in England'. Pevsner's aspirations for the Modern Movement in England were modest because he believed that 'to this day there are two distinct racial types recognizable in England, one tall with long head and long features, little facial display and little gesticulation'. These were art- and innovation-friendly. Pevsner did not actually mention that they were also blond and Aryan, but that was the implication. 'The other round-faced, more agile and more active,' were the 'John Bull' type, though William Hogarth was lumped in with them. 'It is a type less often expressed in art than the other for it often turns against art.' These generalizations are, of course, absurd. Would he have included John Betjeman among the 'round-faced' philistines or would he have escaped by not being agile enough? Pevsner had noticed that this round-faced racial group 'plays far too modest a part in art and architecture'. This was a theory which could have been a great help in selecting student candidates for Birkbeck.

All this nonsense could be excused from an early twentieth-century German steeped in racial anthropology. Rather more disturbing were some points of comparative history. For instance, 'England was far ahead of the rest of Europe at the time of the Venerable Bede.' Ahead of Germany perhaps, but had Pevsner noticed the Byzantine Empire or even Visigoth Spain? Then he claimed that what he called 'babooneries', lively comic depictions in art of playful monkeys, 'originated in England . . . in the middle of the thirteenth century'. Had he never travelled in south-west France, to Poitou or the Saintonge? Monkeys and apes, entwined suggestively with humans, gibber on the capitals and voussoirs of every other Romanesque church. They were a cliché of the age and had appeared on the Gloucester candlestick in England long before the middle of the thirteenth century. And if Pevsner was playing the continental outsider on his pet theme of historicist revival architecture he should not have been claiming that the evocative Gothic revival 'had indeed been explored uncommonly early in England' on the slight evidence of a 1709 Vanbrugh memorandum urging the preservation of the ruins of Woodstock Manor as a park ornament for Blenheim Palace. At that time the French were building an entire revived Gothic cathedral at Orléans, while in Austrian Bohemia, fifty years earlier, Giovanni Santini had built a cathedral-sized Gothic abbey church at Kladruby with a Baroque dome, and a dazzlingly complex Gothic pilgrimage church, the Zelena hora, at Zdar nach Sazavou, this last not much more than a hundred miles from Leipzig, Pevsner's native city.

After these very dubious generalizations Pevsner went on to 1850 and claimed mysteriously that 'By then the great art of English painting was dead altogether – for reasons which can only be understood on a broader basis of cultural changes'. This was only a way of saying, in obscure critical jargon, 'I don't like the Pre-Raphaelites'. Yet Rossetti and his followers fit perfectly into Pevsner's earlier analysis of English painting as being biased towards accurate observation and moral teaching, so why should he have stated that 'the great art of English painting was dead altogether', when in reality it was still developing consistently? But at this point in his lectures Pevsner was building up to a final peroration urging the English, whose conservatism had been a theme of an earlier discourse, to abandon conservatism as something cowardly and unworthy and embrace instead 'the new style'. This he claimed would need courage, but to flatter his listeners he urged that 'right up to a hundred years ago England was the unchallenged pioneer of innovation in technology, industry and commerce'. None of which had any relevance to the proven and enduring qualities of English art and architecture. Pevsner skirted the fact that for the last four centuries English architecture had been historicist and innately conservative, but that explains his lukewarm response to

Elizabethan and Jacobean romanticism and all the architecture descending from Inigo Jones's revived classicism. These two periods of design account for a good four-fifths of the contents of Pevsner's *Buildings of England* and the clear message here is that he did not rate them. He had every right to his aesthetic evaluations, but it is, nevertheless, a profound reservation on the value of his judgements in every book of the series that he either wrote or edited.

Once again the dualism of the man needs to be appreciated. Several times in the Reith Lectures the veil slips and he reveals his admiration for the extreme and his contempt for the compromise. He rebuked A. L. Rowse openly for undervaluing the readiness of both Protestants and Catholics to suffer martyrdom under Queen Mary and Queen Elizabeth, blaming Rowse for 'this absence of understanding for singleness of mind'. For Pevsner the real danger of dabbling in historic revivalist styles was that the architect 'proves not to be driven to express himself in one style and one style only: his own or that of his age. That single-mindedness is lacking, just as it is in Hogarth as a painter.' This explains why he believed Hogarth to be racially 'round-faced'. Here, surely, we are on the lunatic fringe of art criticism, yet this appeared in the heart of a prestigious Reith lecture and in a book published by the Architectural Press. So was Peter Clarke's comic poem overstating the Pevsnerian position? 'Making England responsible for the fancy dress ball of architecture in the Victorian Age', Pevsner continued severely, 'is not complimentary to the aesthetic genius of the nation.' He does not go on to say that all architecture in Europe since the Renaissance has been 'fancy dress', but that has to be the logic of his position and it explains his attention, in each and every entry of his gazetteer, to churches rather than to domestic buildings. The church, if it was Gothic, was pre-fancy dress, structural in its disciplines, like buildings of the Modern Movement. Pevsner in one mood was a tolerant scholar of wide experience; in another a blinkered fanatic for a largely unproven Modernism.

'Conservatism', he complained, as the lectures drew to a close,

> has been demonstrated as a power of long standing in English art.
> Ought one then not to accept the wretched Tudor of suburban
> houses [described in his *Middlesex* as 'a free and comfortable neo-
> Tudor brick architecture which has indeed stood the test of forty
> years splendidly'], the genteel Georgian of wealthier suburban
> houses [like those neo-Georgian houses by Lutyens which he had
> so admired in Hampstead?] and the pompous and petrified
> Classical Re-revival of civic centres, city offices and buildings done
> for the central government right up to the present day as yet
> another sign of a permanent English quality?

The answer to this fiercely rhetorical question was, of course,
supposed to be in the negative; and this was the man who would
in 1963 become the second Chairman of the Victorian Society,
which John Betjeman, more than any other, had brought into
existence. Yet while Pevsner manifestly valued the Victorians
for their engineering he believed that in every other direction,
in art and architecture, the age had been profoundly mistaken.
He could twist most arguments to support his obsession.
Uvedale Price, his guide on matters Picturesque, had actually
complained that Bath lacked picturesque qualities. Yet Pevsner
claimed 'Wren's City of London and the Bath of John Woods
[*sic*] had shown how the Picturesque principles of variety and
surprise, those visual blessings, could be used in urban terms.' To
illustrate his point and England's urban future he offered four
photographs of projected layouts by Sir William Holford and Dr
Leslie Martin, three in the City and one out at Roehampton.
Each one of them relied upon tall blocks, tightly packed and, in
Holford's St Paul's Precinct, ranked geometrically. Pevsner had
persuaded himself that these represented a new urban picturesque. It is not clear that he had the imaginative ability to
realize in his mind's eye how such models would look when
translated into steel and concrete, but here he was, preaching
their adoption from the media pulpit of the nation. He must,
therefore, carry some responsibility for the gross planning
errors, as for the successes, of the next twenty-five years.

The unprecedented reception of Betjeman's *Collected Poems* in 1958 was based upon his two earlier publications in the same decade. *First and Last Loves* of 1952 was a collection of his journalism prefaced with an open attack on 'The Herr Professor-Doktors' and most of it a head-on challenge to everything aesthetic and architectural in which Pevsner believed. *A Few Late Chrysanthemums* of 1954 was a collection of thirty-two poems, deeply conservative and nostalgic in tone. Both books were published by Jock Murray who had supported Betjeman, faithfully and sympathetically, at every turn in his rise to general popular esteem.

In the same triumphant year that the *Collected Poems* were published Betjeman succeeded in launching the Victorian Society, a statutory body with the legal right to be consulted when the alteration or demolition of any significant Victorian building was being proposed. The launch had been effected in a satisfying Establishment style, but then John had been around for quite a long time. As a founder member of the Georgian Group back in the 1930s he knew how to get things done in England. He was a friend of Anne Parsons, not a lady he addressed by a cheeky nickname when he wrote her a letter. As well as being Countess of Rosse by her second marriage to Michael, the 6th Earl, she was Antony Armstrong-Jones's mother by her first marriage and, therefore, Princess Margaret's mother-in-law. On one occasion she and her husband entertained the Betjemans to 'a tiny little dinner party', just them and 'the Happy Couple' as John archly referred to the Royals. That would have impressed him, but what may have weighed even more was the fact that Anne Rosse's London *pied-à-terre*, 18 Stafford Terrace, had the most stunning and completely unaltered Victorian interiors in the capital, decorated and furnished by Lady Rosse's grandfather, the artist Linley Sambourne.

John had written to the Countess on 17 July 1957 proposing an inaugural meeting at her house. Among 'the sort of people we need' were names like H. S. Goodhart-Rendel, John Piper, John

Summerson, Christopher Hussey, Hugh Casson, R. Furneaux Jordan, Kenneth Clark and Lord Mottistone, all predictable enough, but also more unexpected names: J. M. Richards, P. Morton Shand and 'Professor-Doktor Pevsner'. A drinks party for the great, the good and the consciously influential was held in the first-floor drawing-room of No. 18 on 5 November 1957, coincidentally the day the Russians launched the dog Laika in a Sputnik. The party was a success with champagne after the cocktails. Much enthusiasm and some outrage were expressed and Peter Clarke wrote one of his amusing little poems to celebrate the occasion:

> Oh fearful was our task, for evil was the mask
> of Benevolent Authority on Vandalism's face
> when the Betjeman Brigade vowed to start a new crusade
> to preserve Victorian relics from Oblivion and Disgrace.

Clarke referred to Betjeman as 'our Lion-Heart' and obviously saw him as the prime mover in the campaign. Goodhart-Rendel, 'the Father of us All', got into an argument with Hugh Casson who wanted to extend the scope of the proposed Society to include the Edwardians, or even to go up as far as 1951, which might, of course, have included Hugh Casson. Significantly, Nikolaus Pevsner did not attend in person, but he did send a proxy.

When the Victorian Society was actually founded, on 28 February 1958, its stated aim was 'to make sure that the best Victorian buildings and their contents do not disappear before their merits are generally appreciated'. The first Chairman, appointed probably for his experience with the National Trust, was Lord Esher. Anne Rosse and Betjeman were the two Vice-Chairmen, which should have left John well placed to succeed in time the aged Lord Esher. On the committee were Hugh Casson, Mark Girouard, Goodhart-Rendel, Rupert Gunnis, Peter Clarke and Nikolaus Pevsner. To support the new Society Betjeman had managed to drag in, by the sheer force of his personality, Establishment figures like Pevsner, whose attitude to things Victorian has just been considered, and traitors to the style like John Summerson, the value of whose support would later be made clear.

In a letter of 14 June 1966 Betjeman wrote to Summerson appealing for his help to save a threatened railway terminus: 'It is no good my writing about Sir Gilbert and St Pancras in particular', he admitted revealingly,

> because I have been so denigrated by Karl Marx [J. M. Richards] and the Professor-Doktor [Pevsner] as a lightweight wax fruit merchant, I will not carry the necessary guns. K [Kenneth Clark] can't do it, as he is overworked, though his spirit is willing. Now will you? Bung ho, old top, John B.

Summerson flatly refused, in a reply of bloodless academic slyness. 'Every time I look at the building I'm consumed with admiration in the cleverness of the detail,' Summerson wrote, 'and every time I leave it I wonder why as a whole it is so nauseating.' His conclusion was: 'I shall hate to see all that gorgeous detail being hacked down but I really don't think one could go to a Minister and say this is a great piece of architecture, a great national monument.' Summerson had written a definitive and sensitive book on the architecture of Georgian London and had nothing in mind that might replace a demolished St Pancras, yet he felt able to make that profoundly ungenerous response to Betjeman's appeal on behalf of one of the most memorable urban features of a threatened capital. Summerson's reply deserves to be remembered as an indictment of the strange intolerance which characterized so many advocates of the Modern Movement.

Betjeman's letter, quoted above, illustrates what a chip he had on his shoulder about his academic status *vis-à-vis* the architectural establishment. This was nothing new. In the early 1950s he had complained bitterly to James Lees-Milne, 'I travel third and am cut by people who count and looked down upon by the new refugee "scholars" who have killed all we like by their "research" – i.e. Nikolaus Pevsner that dull pedant from

Prussia.' And that was written in 1952, long before the *Pevsners*
had become a national institution. Such complaints and expres-
sions of dejected self-pity have, however, to be treated with
caution. For all his usual exuberance John sometimes enjoyed
the feeling of being under-appreciated. In one remarkable
letter of 25 June 1971 to his latest lady confidante, Mary Wilson,
the wife of the Prime Minister, he complained piteously about
the personal malice of the literary world and of how he
suffered 'even under people who pretend to be friends (e.g. John
Piper and his wife) who feel, one knows, that one is "trivial"
and not "important"'. That was an extraordinary claim to
make about two of his closest friends. But the truth behind his
feeling was, if he was ever honestly analytical, that he laughed
and joked far too much for his own good. Laughter frightens
insecure people. They feel more confident with a grave and
serious face; laughter suggests that perhaps nothing is entirely
serious. A Vice-Chairman may be allowed to giggle and joke
and fool around, but when it comes to appointing a Chairman,
then the Lord Eshers of life are called upon, and the Nikolaus
Pevsners.

This was what Betjeman had always been up against, his own
irrepressible sense of the ridiculous. But now, with his populist
image, created by any number of short television programmes
and broadcasts in the preceding decade, he could at least muster
support to outface the philistine Modernists and state the
obvious – that nothing likely to replace the spires and arches of
St Pancras would come anywhere near it in visual values.
Conservation would become a national crusade in opposition to
this 'treason of clerks' by men like Summerson and Pevsner,
acolytes of a dreary and unproven faith of the 1930s that had
revived and flourished after the traumas of war and during post-
war economic stress. Betjeman became famous at a mean and
unsatisfying time for his country, when most direction in the
arts was pretentious, wilfully obscure or wrong. What made him
such a force in the 1950s was not simply his genius with words,
but his huge delight in using that genius to insist that ordinary

places and ordinary emotions were subtle and important, and that what we inherited we should keep.

Any mention of a religious faith in such a context always brings a chill into the air and an upward rolling of the eyes, but in John Betjeman's case it is inescapable. Throughout his life John was a deeply convinced and practising Christian. There are lines in a poem by the Caroline divine George Herbert that claim that anyone who simply sweeps a room in God's name is carrying out an act of Grace. Herbert was an Anglican, but his was a very Catholic belief, one exemplified in the life of St Teresa of Lisieux, who died when she was barely out of adolescence after a life of simple convent drudgery, vowing to spend her time in Heaven doing good upon Earth, responding to the prayers of the Faithful and accompanying such acts occasionally with the perfume of roses. It all sounds simplistic and naïve but at the heart of it is a Christian pantheism that sees God in every aspect of life, and it was this pantheism that Betjeman brought up to date with inevitable consequences for environmental matters. Piper had completed his conversion that day in Whittington Station in 1939, but he had been finding his way to a broader appreciation of the material fabric of life for several years.

Included in his *First and Last Loves* is one brash and foolish article, 'Antiquarian Prejudice', based on a lecture he had given to the Group Theatre in 1937. In substance it is a rehash of *Ghastly Good Taste*, a long diatribe against all things architectural in the modern world with no positive conclusion or way out at the end of it. Pevsner never wrote anything half as silly. But it does open with a bold statement of this Christian pantheism which Piper was soon to refine and direct:

> I come to you fresh from Evensong and with my outlook widened. Architecture has a wider meaning than that which is commonly given to it. For architecture means not a house, or a single building or a church, or Sir Herbert Baker, or the glass at Chartres, but your surroundings; not a town or a street, but our whole over-populated island. It is concerned with where we eat, work, sleep, play, congregate, escape. It is our background, often too permanent.

By the 1950s he had become even more confident and far more potent. He still did not know what the style solution was in the way of future building, but he had seen that what the developers had borrowed from Pevsner's Modern Movement was making things worse than they had been before: therefore conservation was the first policy. Our existing environment, the result of unplanned accretions over the centuries, had enormous charm if only we could stand aside from doctrinal assumptions and appreciate it. Aesthetic conservatism and practical conservation were positive forces.

Almost every poem in that 1958 *Collected* edition relates to this theme of a new visual appreciation. They can be divided into three moods, or would Nikolaus have called them 'categories'? One is openly devout, one revealingly personal and one entertainingly descriptive. But they all reflect joy or sorrow in an actual English environment and in ordinary English lives. They assert, by their concrete detail and real place-names, that suburbs and seaside towns, road-houses and stations are not simply worthwhile subjects for poetry, but significant sectors of Creation. It is the 'sweeping a room for God' idea widened to include popular architecture, popular commerce, popular living. All these poems communicate without a shadow of modish literary obscurity or free verse; and that in itself has never improved Betjeman's standing in the world of literary criticism, where the critics depend upon obscurities to earn their keep.

Betjeman's occasional long poems in rhyming couplets, written deliberately to air environmental concerns – 'The Town Clerk's Views', 'The Dear Old Village' and 'The Village Inn' – were never his most effective proselytizing vehicles. His satire is too knockabout, with wicked developers like Farmer Whistle and 'his doxy in the nearest town' and his voice on 'the War Ag. Committee'. That Town Clerk with his belief that Cambridge 'needs more factories, not useless things/Like that great chapel which they keep at King's', is too outrageous to be credible. It is when Betjeman uses popular themes – Page Three Girls and sensational accidents – but with his heart involved and his metres light and tripping, that he makes a real environment unexpectedly important. A whole string of poems are really versified concentrations of material which would have made an entry in a *Shell Guide*. In 'Business Girls', the London glimpsed from railway trains entering Paddington – 'At the back precarious bathrooms/Jutting out from upper floors' – is evoked to create a delicate parallelism between the shoddy conversions of old houses – 'frail partitions', 'draughty skylight', 'Waste pipes chuckle into runnels' – and the vulnerability of the single secretary girls who occupy them. The result is both aphrodisiac and protective, pure Betjeman morally, pure NW1 environmentally. In 'Essex' he brushes aside the lost idyll of 'cottage doors and hollyhocks' to reveal the realities of an expanding capital city: 'huge and convoluted pubs' and a 'half-land of football clubs'. In 'Middlesex' that potential Page Three Girl, Elaine, daintily alighting from 'the red electric train' in Ruislip Gardens, wallows in named commercial products – Jacqmar scarf, Windsmoor, Drene and Innoxa – then 'settles down to sandwich supper and the television screen'. With audience empathy secured, Betjeman tilts the whole poem upward to 'Low laburnum-leaned-on railings' and the 'scent of mayfields' to assert what has been lost and insist upon an historic continuity. Elaine and the 'lost Elysium – rural Middlesex' both matter, they are parts of a comprehensible, enjoyable togetherness: recent past and lovingly, lasciviously observed present. Where T. S. Eliot's warped imagination saw himself in 'The Waste Land' as one of these secretary girls, drearily seduced and then abandoned, Betjeman lusts after them on one superficial level and on another sees them as happy, conventional figures in this new, shallow, yet perfectly valid, suburban civilization. One poet neurotically writhes; the other cheerfully embraces modernity.

Being the poet of the specific has its dangers – it can result in bathos – but Betjeman embraces embarrassment as a life-enhancing quality and he draws God into it deliberately. When he is riding piously high in 'A Lincolnshire Church' with its sanctuary lamp for the Reserved Sacrament – 'There where the white light flickers,/Our Creator is with us yet' – he switches abruptly, 'To be worshipped by you and the woman/Of the slacks and the cigarette'. In 'Christmas' he ends devoutly – 'God was man in Palestine/And lives to-day in Bread and Wine' – but only four lines earlier he is writing about 'Bath salts and inexpensive scent/And hideous tie so kindly meant'.

For me his greatest poem is 'Pershore Station, or A Liverish Journey First Class' where the title is exactly specific and everything depends upon a sense of place, history and informed awareness. Betjeman was returning from a visit to Penelope, his wife, from whom he was by now amicably separated, when introspection set in. His train was standing in Pershore Station. Perhaps he sensed that isolation that travel can impose and all the social humbug of a first-class compartment,

> When sudden the waiting stillness shook with the ancient spells
> Of an older world than all our worlds in the sound of the
> > Pershore bells.
> They were ringing them down for Evensong in the lighted
> > abbey near,
> Sounds which had poured through apple boughs for seven
> > centuries here.

He was using Lord Macaulay and G. K. Chesterton's jogging anapaestic rhythms, the technical 'ringing down' for that uncertain jangle that begins all campanology as mathematics searches for a pattern, then making it more precise by the 'apple boughs' of the Vale of Evesham and the 'seven' of the centuries. 'Guilt, Remorse, Eternity' follow with that Betjemanian frankness of 'plunged in a deep self pity I dreamed of another wife/And lusted for freckled faces and lived a separate life'. It is a confessional, with the twentieth century's social failures suggested from one particular experience in one particular time and place.

Betjeman captured his wider readership by two entirely superficial, affectionately accurate poems – 'Hunter Trials' and 'How to Get On in Society' – then carried them deep into more adult territory. Has any other English poet written up his life, lusts, loves and losses with quite such openness? Perhaps we are still too near in time to appreciate how he turned that exhibitionism, that holy transparency, into a popular media personality of serious stature. It was as if a Restoration poet, some bawdy, leering Rochester, was able to transform himself into a humble country parson poet, like William Cowper, at will. In the *Collected Poems* 'Senex' and 'Olney Hymns' are set on opposite pages. On the left is Betjeman the uninhibited: 'Your teeth are stuffed with underwear,/Suspenders torn asunder there/And buttocks in your paws!'; while on the right-hand page is, 'O God the Olney Hymns abound/With words of Grace which Thou didst choose'.

It is revealing that in T. S. Eliot and John Betjeman's lifetimes Anglican intellectuals almost invariably rated Eliot far above Betjeman. Eliot had nothing he was ever willing to confess and only sonorous paradoxes to offer, while Betjeman lived life to the full, wrote out most of its details memorably and went at least part way to converting a philistine nation to something which it then christened 'Heritage' and half destroyed. The Church of England has never plucked up the confidence to make saints as the Catholics do. This is probably fortunate as by now we would be saddled with the most appalling gallery of old compromisers, political to a man and woman. But if it ever had the nerve to canonize, what a patron saint of the Environment John would have made, spending his Heaven, a little like St Teresa, rescuing endangered buildings on Earth, rewarding positive souls with good company and diffusing occasionally, if not the perfume of roses, then the more subtle scents of hassocks, old incense and oil-lamps.

CHAPTER EIGHT

The Last Battles of the Old Warriors

It is difficult not to admire Pevsner for the way in which he kept his powder dry and his dignity intact when Betjeman was slipping into unashamedly racist insults. John had histrionically entitled the foreword to his 1952 *First and Last Loves* as 'Love is dead', and ended a petulant account of England's degenerate condition with:

> The Herr-Professor-Doktors are writing everything down for us, sometimes throwing in a little hurried pontificating too, so we need never bother to feel or think or see again. We can eat our Weetabix, catch the 8.48, read the sports column and die; for love is dead.

And, as if that was not quite enough malice and spite for one chapter, he quoted, from the *Book of Common Prayer*, one of Cranmer's great appeals for Charity, 'the very bond of peace and of all virtues' to add religious hypocrisy to injury.

Nikolaus simply ignored the thrusts. When it was relevant in an article to mention Betjeman's name his references were scholarly and polite, vaguely approving, with just a shade of condescension as from one older man to someone younger who was doing his best. The only piece of Betjeman's writing he ever affected to notice publicly was that *Ghastly Good Taste*. Even this he described as 'memorable', but only for the typographical experiments on its title page. He understood that Betjeman had been 'an undergraduate at Oxford'; there was no mention of the painful fact that he had never become a graduate at Oxford.

In their very different ways both men had found secure niches in the Establishment hierarchy. John was an official, lovable rogue, Nikolaus the reliable deliverer of appropriate judgements. Pevsner, with his well-known stylistic viewpoints, had even begun to feature in the satirical columns of *Private Eye* in a running intellectual football match with regular fortnightly fixtures on the lines of: Trebetherick Rovers 1, Neasden Town 0 (*Baldy Pevsner, own goal*). Neither image expressed a complete truth, but that was unimportant. They both made steady progress up the honours ladder which would lead, so impartially and judiciously, to a knighthood for each in the same year, 1969. As a taster Nikolaus got his CBE in 1953; John had to wait for the same honour until 1960. But in the same year as his CBE John was awarded the Queen's Medal for Poetry while Nikolaus would have to wait until 1967 to receive the RIBA Gold Medal for Architecture. John could be said to have won out in the end with the Laureateship in 1972. Only a seat in the Lords for Nikolaus could have trumped that; but with his influential position on so many committees and commissions – Royal Fine Arts, Redundant Churches, Historic Buildings Council – and with Modernism of one kind or another becoming the urban vernacular, Pevsner should have been a very happy man.

Apparently he was not. Although historicism of the kind he had fought against had become a joke and only a few provincial architects like Raymond Erith were still managing to design modest classical country houses for conservative clients, Pevsner had, like some New England witch-finder of old, sniffed out a new threat, a most unexpected heresy. Expressionism was back again, running like wildfire through new building ventures in countries right around the world. The old enemy of Bauhaus purity in the 1920s had risen once more and Pevsner saw this as 'historicism' in yet another disguise. Contemporary architects were picking up from buildings of the Twenties and Thirties all the little Expressionist tricks that masked honest functional form and asserted the individuality of the designer – something that the Bauhaus school of architecture had abhorred. Pevsner complained of 'the random rubble racket', and 'canopies which curl up, or do a Hitler salute, or snake off to the left or right, and in fact do anything they can do to avoid a straightforward statement of what a canopy is actually built for'.

Pevsner was so upset and angered by this, to him, regressive development that, most uncharacteristically, he published in the *RIBA Journal* a long, fascinatingly illustrated article, first given as a lecture, attacking most of the best-known living architects. He called it 'The Return of Historicism'. It is a most revealing work and it fills out and confirms most of the conclusions about Pevsner's mind-set, the basic flaw in his critical sensibility, that earlier chapters have been circling. But before considering it in more detail it will be timely to recall what was happening in the real world of British architecture and design while Pevsner was tying himself into polemical knots over the heresy of Expressionism.

His enchantingly absurd, irrelevant and quickly forgotten article came out in 1961. This was at the height of the conservation battles being fought in England. Between 1961 and 1962 the Euston Arch, the most fiercely contested monument of all, was not only demolished but also, despite the contractor's offer to number its stones for re-erection and despite the fact that it would have fitted superbly into the new proposed Euston layout, ground down into small pieces to make rockeries. And the Euston Arch was not the only casualty. A few months later the Coal Exchange in the City went the same way, and that was not simply a vast and beautiful Victorian interior, it was an example of that Victorian engineering vision which Nikolaus Pevsner claimed to admire and value. But who was in the forefront of the battle to save it? Not Pevsner, but Betjeman. It can fairly be said that in these exciting years of national debate Pevsner no longer had his eye on the ball. On what, then, was his eye fixed?

'The Return of Historicism' opened with an expression of

wounded personal betrayal. It would be hypocritical at this point to pretend to any serious sympathy with Nikolaus on this issue. His new role as the frustrated Savonarola of Wildwood Terrace has more comedy about it than tragedy. But his rage after so many years of impersonal calm is interesting since it reveals the very strict limits to which he believed the Modern Movement should be confined.

Rehearsing the past, Pevsner reverently recorded that as the twentieth century dawned and the Art Nouveau wilted away 'there arose a generation of giants, who created a new style of architecture entirely independent of the past'. Had all those links which he had claimed to find in his *Pioneers* with Voysey and Morris been so much eyewash, delivered to soothe English susceptibilities? 'One might have thought', Pevsner continued reproachfully, 'one had a right to assume historicism was at an end.' Did he really believe that historic revivalism had, as far as architecture was concerned, been consigned to the dustbin? As he understood it, the principle of this new architecture was that form must strictly follow function. A building 'should have nothing on its exterior to reduce its well functioning'. It should look exactly like what it was meant to be and nothing more. Curiously the author-editor of the *Buildings of England* seems not to have considered what should happen if a building was meant to be ornamental, escapist, cosily domestic or magisterially impressive. How should a building bring you to your knees or express the wealth and taste of its owner? It has to be assumed that as the contented inhabitant of 2 Wildwood Terrace, Pevsner had no wish to see any owner's wealth or taste expressed in his home and certainly no desire to be brought to his knees. He had learnt his stylistic creed long ago, in Germany in the 1920s. Later, that moral steel had been forged anew, in the long years of austerity and rationing of wartime and Socialist Britain.

What particularly vexed Pevsner now was the way in which the exteriors of buildings were being designed with – and here in the Pevsnerian syntax the key word can easily be lost – 'an expression which does not convey a sense of confidence in their well functioning'. 'Expression' was the word, and it was Expressionism that mild, scholarly Pevsner actively hated: when the outward face of a structure was designed to convey its architect's emotions rather than the building's function. What was doubly sinful was this 'Return of Historicism'. Jörn Utzon, instead of inventing his own Expressionist devices, had gone back to a 1919 design for an Art Centre by Hermann Finsterlin to borrow the dramatic, sail-like roofline for his 1968 Sydney Opera House. John Johansen had taken the Expressionist form of his 1959–64 American Embassy in Dublin from Gaudí's block of flats, the Casa Milá, Barcelona, of 1905–10.

One curious feature of Pevsner's anger was that it was second-hand. He owed these two perceptions of an insidious return of Modernist historicism, and several others even less convincing, to articles in the *Architectural Review* of 1959 and *The Listener* of 1960 by Reyner Banham. He was, as usual, absolutely open about his borrowings. Dr Banham, the architectural journalist, was on Betjeman's hit-list. 'Reyner Banham, thank God, has left the country,' he wrote to Jock Murray in 1964. Then, when he was collecting articles for a proposed polemical book on building outrages, he wrote with his usual, cheerful malice, 'I should like to dedicate the book to Reyner Banham, Dr Pevsner and Michael Manser [a later RIBA President].' But then, having second thoughts, he went back and crossed Pevsner's name out. They were, after all, both distinguished members of the Victorian Society, technically fighting on the same side.

Pevsner's problem, which he would not have seen as such, was that he remained, for the last fifty years of his life, trapped in a time-warp. As he admitted frankly in an address of 1963, 'doubts often torture me today, being an inveterate functionalist of the thirties'. He was proud of his inability to move with the times. For him a Platonic perfection of architectural design had been achieved in those far-off pre-war days. He would remain throughout his life a believer in the mystique of the Bauhaus.

Unfortunately he had adopted the Bauhaus ideals at precisely the time when buildings were learning to do just about everything except fly. They could very nearly reach the clouds; they could span huge spaces effortlessly with a thin shell of concrete, realize the designer's wildest fantasies, control light and minimalize down to a hair's breadth. Yet Pevsner was determined to deny all this for no better reason than that several decades earlier the distressed economies of the Weimar Republic had dictated, for a ten-year period, a puritanical simplicity. This has always to be remembered: behind that mild exterior and blameless lifestyle Pevsner was a convert, he was 'born again'; everything else, all his sophisticated awareness of the mutation of the classical orders – Mannerism, Palladianism, neo-Classicism – was just for the birds. This certainty of belief must have given him a great feeling of self-confidence and superiority. There he was, the virtual Dean of Britain's architectural establishment, with no architectural training but generally respected and deferred to by the planners of this brash, under-educated, half-socialist, half-capitalist state, and whatever else he had to say, do or write, secure within his mind was this Bauhaus truth. An outsider's role can sometimes be a happy one.

When I talked to Pevsner's elder son, Dieter, I pressed him several times for his father's views on celebrated contemporary architects such as Basil Spence, Maxwell Fry or Berthold Lubetkin, all of whom he must have seen as rampant Expressionist heretics. Dieter told me that his father 'was always interested, even if he didn't like their buildings'. He had 'great respect' for James Stirling, the same for Denys Lasdun. A typical remark of his would be: 'I'm sure there's a reason for all this, but I hate it.' He had no patience with modern designs that were only a kind of self-aggrandizement, what might be called 'personality architecture'. He looked in buildings for modesty and good manners.

It was in 1963 that his wife Lola died very suddenly, leaving him, by most accounts, a changed man. He continued to live at 2 Wildwood Terrace, but with a warmly supportive family close by. Writing was done in the kitchen on an electric typewriter, but he was not interested in cooking. Supper would be taken usually with his daughter, Uta, in No. 1 next door. Tomas lived in No. 11 and Dieter in the adjacent Wildwood Grove at No. 5. Sometimes, if he had forgotten where he was supposed to be, he would have supper twice. Entertaining had never been a priority with the Pevsners. There would be one week set apart in the year for returning dinner invitations, and a stream of guests arriving every night. Some, according to legend, were greeted at the door by a worried Nikolaus with 'You're not supposed to be here until Tuesday!' He was much more the reserved, absent-minded professor than the scholar of iron and steel. For a time after Lola's death the family were worried that he might lose the will to complete his *Buildings of England*. But Dieter got him back on the road again to continue his counties, driving him up and down Hampshire. Yet some of his quiet inner joy at work well done had gone and this could explain the remote role he played in subsequent years as the conservation wars raged and hardly a week passed without his rival appearing on a television screen or writing persuasively to the converted in the *Daily Telegraph*.

Betjeman's 'Causeries' for that paper included 'Size without Greatness', an attack on London city office blocks; 'The Best and Worst of an Era', Sheffield's Victorian and modern suburbs compared, much in favour of the former; 'Destruction of a City', Peterborough's disastrous twentieth-century expansion; 'Temple to the Age of Steam', an impassioned defence of St Pancras; and 'Keeping against the Odds', on small town streetscapes (he used Wantage) under threat from developers. All of them were trenchant: some like 'Contemprikit', or how to design your own modern building, were tellingly funny with a vicious analysis of mosaic cladding and the art of placing all your components off-centre.

Pevsner's writing career revived in the lonely years after Lola's death. *Sources of Modern Art* was published in 1964, *Some Architectural Writers of the Nineteenth Century* in 1972 and, last of all, *A History of Building Types* in 1976. Those were in addition to the remaining *Buildings of England*, the last of which came out in 1974. Between 1968 and 1969 he also served as Slade Professor of Fine Art at Oxford, so it would be wrong to think that his later academic years were in any sense a decline.

For a full account of Betjeman's hyperactivities in the 1960s, his golden decade of fame, fortune and, as far as an outsider can judge, of love, it is essential to read the second of the two volumes of Betjeman's letters edited by his daughter, Candida Lycett Green. The first volume is good, but the second is truly definitive. It opens in 1951, by which time his editor was already an alert, affectionate and acutely observant daughter. This means that the introductory chapters which she wrote, in between the six- or seven-year groupings of letters, are better informed than anything even a scholarly and sympathetic biographer could hope to achieve. Her confidence that her father's life would shine through a generous selection of his correspondence, including some letters that a nervous editor might have censored, was entirely justified. By this bold stroke of publishing we have been given the entire man, a positive poet in a largely negative world. Candida has lived up to her name.

She estimates that, in the 1960s alone, her father must have made over fifty films for television: films on London byways, films on early cinemas, on country houses where he played the genial second to antiques experts, on the Holy Land, other poets' lives, Britain from the air, market towns revisited and, unavoidably after that 'Elaine' poem, on lost rural Middlesex, the Lyonesse of the home counties. The effect of all these relaxed and entertaining half-hour slots on the nation's environmental awareness cannot be calculated. But, just as the *Antiques Roadshow* has given everyone an eye for potential quality, making life difficult for predatory dealers, so all those viewers who grew familiar with that laughing crumpled face, the kindly eyes and the battered hat have become aware of the value of old buildings and the need to be alert to the threat of the developer. Concrete lamp standards have never recovered from Betjeman's contempt. Every traveller can now savour the

Victorian chic of a great London terminus, relish Liverpool Street's forest of iron Gothic arches and look down on the blandness of Waterloo (Eurostar platforms excepted). Betjeman, single-handed, raised the nation's level of visual sophistication by several points.

People remember his championing of the Victorians, but of more influence on our visual awareness has been his affectionate and challenging appraisal of twentieth-century domestic design: our semi-detached land and superior detached villadom. He made the revolutionary but entirely plausible suggestion that the average row of 1920s and 1930s suburban villas has as much architectural interest as any equally average Georgian terrace and often rather more. This is an assessment which has still to be taken on board by the Heritage Industry. If and when it is ever accepted, that will set up an interesting storm of re-listing and of preservation orders.

Betjeman's early television programmes concentrated on people, fat ladies by the seaside and ageing music-hall stars, with only a light architectural subtext. There was a feature on Clevedon which afforded hardly a glimpse of the town's rich stock of villas, Regency to Moderne, but laid much emphasis on belligerent old ladies eating their dinners in retirement homes to John's sympathetic voice-over. Later ventures like his 'Metroland', covering a broad swathe of North London, were more ambitious, with buildings prominent and humanity an amusing cast of extras.

The programme was threaded ingeniously along the Underground's Metropolitan Line from Baker Street out to Verney Junction in rural Buckinghamshire. It should be seen as a generous tribute to Pooterism, decentralization and all the unfashionable bourgeois values. John drew freely on the techniques of those first *Shell Guides* – humour, hints of the supernatural, folklore and an appreciative response to neglected detail, with sex as a lubricious extra. Over decorous shots of early nineteenth-century stuccoed houses he intoned with prurient relish:

There, walled in from public view, lived the kept women. What Puritan arms have stretched within these rooms to touch what tender breasts, as the cab-horse stamped in the road outside? Sweet, secret suburb on the city's rim: St John's Wood!

On the very edge of poetry, such prose lent a sensuous undertone to fretted bargeboards and Regency Gothic windows. Later, to the accompaniment of his usual mockery of Harrow school, Betjeman waved his arms to demand attention to rows of Harrow's suburban houses which no other commentator would have dreamt of including. First came a defiantly angular Ruskinian street of about 1880 and then, most telling, against shots of lawns being mown and cars washed, 'the show-houses of the newly-built estates, a younger, brighter, homelier Metroland'. Reciting their names, 'Rose Lea, Rose Mount, Rose Roof', Betjeman sold their charms to his viewers, many of whom would have lived in similar houses: 'each one is slightly different to the next, a bastion of individual taste on fields that once were bright with buttercups'. Yet the implication was that something more aesthetically valuable had replaced those buttercup fields. Betjeman was reversing trite Wordsworthian pre-conceptions. A sequence dwelling on the stained glass of the porches with swallows, galleons and rustic scenes in leaded lights consolidated the lesson of values.

Conventionally historic buildings did feature as the Metropolitan moved out into Hertfordshire. There was Norman Shaw's Grims Dyke with John stumbling up the dark stairs and demanding, 'Have I strayed into a Hitchcock film?' only to end up in a meeting of a ladies' Luncheon Club. Inevitably he visited Voysey's own house, The Orchard, treating it delicately with a masterly absence of condescending didacticism, each wrought-iron detail enjoyed rather than taught. Eventually, out at Amersham, Betjeman could not resist one of those Modern Movement houses which he had always avoided in the past, Amyas Connell's 1931 High and Over, 'a concrete house in the shape of a letter Y'. But what he could resist was any hint of unreserved praise:

'I am the home of a twentieth-century family', it proclaims, 'that loves air and sunlight and open country'. It started a style called Moderne, perhaps rather old-fashioned today, and one day, poor thing, it woke up and found developers in its back garden. Goodbye *H*igh hopes and *O*ver-confidence.

His gently malicious comments were delivered over camera shots of dull flats and new houses crowding up to High and Over's garden hedge. But, though to the unprejudiced eye the superiority of Connell's aggressively geometrical elevations to those of the developers' flats was manifest, there was not a note of regret in Betjeman's words.

He was never an amateur natural who had strayed into the TV studio but always, ever since television broadcasts began, a professional. In his nature the technician balanced out the literary man; lighting, angles and cutting fascinated him. He took on more and more work, not only for the platform it gave and the money it brought, but for the company, the team-work it offered him. The average journalist who goes into television has confidence; Betjeman had confidence and much more, a relaxed and yet controlled eccentricity, enormous background knowledge of his subjects and an apparently vulnerable charm. Though he was such a sincere snob, he himself appeared classless. With that gently bleating voice and the earnestness that followed quickly in the wake of laughter, he could get away with any opinion, however outrageous. This was everyone's favourite uncle mellowing into the wisdom of old age. In the 1970s, by his sheer omnipresence, Betjeman drew ahead of Pevsner. Betjeman on the Isle of Man, Betjeman on the Isle of Wight, Betjeman visits Australia (and loved it!); 'Thank God its Sunday', 'A Passion for Churches', 'Metroland'. As his poetic creativity dwindled, his gift for presenting himself became more sure. Old age was the prime of his life, for he was one of those people who are born to be old, the wise sage of the nation-tribe.

Pevsner, on the other hand, should have been permanently forty-five, middle-aged and serious. With the image of

Betjeman – jolly, unpretentious and permanently benign – still so strong, it comes almost as a relief to remember the dry, unyielding integrity of Nikolaus who was no one's particular favourite, the expert who never played to the gallery. For me he is forever the architectural historian of icy certainty whom Paul Rudolph invited to open the building that Rudolph himself had designed to house his very own School of Art and Architecture at Yale. Pevsner marched straight into Rudolph's hysterically Expressionist block and asked his distinguished audience: 'What do we see here?' Then, before they could answer, he told them: 'Massive piers of concrete rise. Projections are over-emphasised throughout. Heavy slabs are crossed by thin slabs. Spaces inside cross too and offer sequences of most dramatic effects inside the building and even out of it.'

He was giving them a typical *Buildings of England* treatment out there in Connecticut, but this time he went on to his conclusion and told them all exactly why he did not think much of the building he had been brought expensively across the Atlantic to open. Was it not too personal, too exciting, too powerful a stimulant for the students who would work there? He warned them, 'woe to him who imitates Paul Rudolph', then added further woe to anyone who imitated Saarinen, Philip Johnson or Yamasaki. It was a performance of acid honesty and it might well have been Hannes Meyer himself, risen from the ashes of the Bauhaus, standing there addressing them. As a soothing gesture he did suggest that since Rudolph had designed the place for Rudolph to work in, everything might be all right. But later, in a typical note of righteous self-congratulation, he added a postscript to the published address, noting that Rudolph, like Gropius all those years ago, had soon left the school to concentrate on private practice, so the whole project, as he had prophesied, had been a big mistake: 'this demonstrates', he wrote, 'the necessity of neutral designs for neutral buildings'. It was a conclusion which should have been engraved on his headstone in Clyffe Pypard churchyard, but being Pevsner, he only allowed his name and dates on that.

Death continued the curious, satisfying parallelism of the two lives. Both men suffered the slow decline of Parkinson's disease. The faithful are supposed to pray for such a lingering illness so that they can have time to compose their souls appropriately and John did just that. Anyone who is interested in a death-bed scene, written with the sureness of touch of a latter-day Dickens, should read the last pages of Candida Lycett Green's second volume – sunshine on a May morning in Trebetherick, the sound of the sea in the Camel estuary, his beloved nursery animals, Archie and Jumbo, disposed whimsically about him and loving friends gathered. If anyone deserved a good end John Betjeman did, and he got one. It is very moving. I like best the touch of Stanley the cat, fast asleep on the bed and indifferent to it all as cats tend to be.

Nikolaus's last years were less lyrical. After a heart-attack he had a fall, breaking his thighbone. The three operations required to pin it resulted in brain damage. He never walked again and never wrote. Betjeman's daughter insists that in their last years the two old men became quite harmonious in their relations. I prefer to emphasize their conflict as that was more real. Whether either of them had the answer to Britain's architectural ills is doubtful. Pevsner would have been happy to see the country fill up with neutral buildings for a neutral people, and that is what is still happening. Betjeman put most of his faith in the goodness of what we had got already, and, if he did not want the clock put back, then he wanted the hands to stop moving. Did both of them die too soon for their own satisfaction? Would they have been delighted by the Big Three – James Stirling, Norman Foster and Richard Rogers? My bet is that Pevsner would have given Foster ten out of ten for elegance and good manners perfectly combined, but for Foster's own offices on the Thames at Battersea, not for Stansted Airport. The spiritless perfection of that office structure would have been for Pevsner the Bauhaus ideal carried to the ultimate. Betjeman, I suspect, would have mocked Rogers's Lloyd's Building in the City but liked it for the photo-opportunities it offered on all those balconies. Stirling's Stuttgart museum and art gallery would have gone down well with Archibald Ormsby-Gore, and there would have been film clips to prove it.

They are both gone now to the quiet earth of village church-yards, Pevsner with only his family and a few friends at the funeral, but a memorial service in the Catholic Apostolic Church in London's Gordon Square for a wider congregation and Alec Clifton-Taylor giving an appreciative address. Betjeman went with more drama. On that bizarre May after-noon when six bearers in Victorian black trundled his coffin across the dunes to St Enodoc for burial, all the media folk, camera teams and reporters had been asked to assemble in the slight shelter of the lychgate. They say it was lucky that the rain was belting down remorselessly from the low Cornish clouds because almost everyone in that blasé, seen-it-all-before group was streaming tears. It was right that they should have been, because he was not only a poet, he was also one of them.

Index

Index

Index

Index

Index

Marlborough Downs, 1
Marlow, 118
MARS group, 46
Martin, Leslie, 146
Marylebone: St Cyprian's church, 126
Maufe, Sir Edward, 16
Mead, The (house), Wantage, 7
Mendelsohn, Erich, 35
Mereworth Castle, Kent, 142
'Metroland' (JB; TV programme), 164–6
Meyer, Hannes, 9, 167
Mid Eastern Wales (Vyvyan Rees; *Shell Guide*), 122
Mid Western Wales (Vyvyan Rees; *Shell Guide*), 122
'Middlesex' (JB; poem), 153, 163
Middlesex (NP; *Buildings of England*), 113, 125, 129, 146
Mies van der Rohe, Ludwig, 9, 93
'Model Housing for the Working Classes' (NP; article), 105
Modernism: NP's commitment to, 9, 18, 78, 84–6, 90–2, 94, 96, 108, 115, 132, 145, 152, 159, 168; JB's attitude to, 18, 35, 42, 44–5, 48–9, 150, 166; Hastings promotes, 22, 27; NP writes on, 30, 80–6, 90–1, 94, 140, 143; Waugh satirizes, 35–6; MARS group supports, 46; houses, 50; Shand plans series on origins of, 80–3
Monet, Claude, 86
Morris, May, 28, 95
Morris, William: Paul Nash overlooks, 27; JB admires, 28–9, 46, 48; in historical continuity, 30, 159; works towards Art Nouveau, 42; JB criticizes, 48; NP on, 82, 84, 86, 88, 95, 106, 124; Mackmurdo on, 96; on Bedford Park, 130
Mortimer, Raymond, 25
Mottistone, John Seely, Baron, 148
Mount Zion (JB; poetry collection), 18, 49, 59–60
Munch, Edvard: *The Scream*, 87
Murray, John ('Jock'), 100, 110, 113, 138, 147, 160

Murray, John (publisher): County Guides, 110–11, 113, 117–18, 122

Nairn, Ian, 123
Nash, John, 73
Nash, Paul, 26, 31, 36–7, 51, 57, 73–4
'Nautical Style, The': Piper expounds on, 97–8
Nazism, 77–8, 81
Neale, J. P., 61
New Delhi, 24
Newman, John, 121, 123–4, 135
Newton Road (No. 32), London, 50
Nicholson, Ben, 51
Norman architecture, 7–8, 48
Northamptonshire (Lady Juliet Smith; *Shell Guide*), 136–7
Northcliffe, Alfred Harmsworth, Viscount, 21
Northumberland and Durham (Thomas Sharp; *Shell Guide*), 57, 73
Norwood, Cyril: *The English Tradition of Education*, 24
Nottinghamshire (NP; *Buildings of England*), 113

Old Lights for New Chancels (JB; poems), 59, 110
Old Rectory, Farnborough, Berkshire, 3
Olivier, Edith, 72, 74, 120, 135
'Olney Hymns' (JB; poem), 155
'Omega' (NP; article), 106
Omega Workshop, 99
'Our Padre' (JB; poem), 89
'Outer Suburbs, The' (JB; poem), 59
Outline of European Architecture (NP), 99, 111
Oxford University: JB at, 19, 33
Oxon (Piper; *Shell Guide*), 57–8, 74, 97

Pakenham Hall, Ireland (*now* Tullynally Castle), 18
Pangbourne, Berkshire, 118
'Passing of the Village, The' (JB; article), 43–5

Index

Piper, John (*cont.*)
  Architectural Review, 83, 97–9,
    101–2, 104, 116; topographical
    perceptions and descriptions, 95,
    96–9, 106; background, 96–7; as war
    artist, 99; and JB's rivalry with NP,
    100, 137; aesthetic values, 101–3, 105,
    108, 117–19; disparages NP, 113;
    collaborates on *Murray's Guides*,
    117–18; rivalry with NP, 117; and
    launching of Victorian Society, 147;
    JB accuses of despising, 150; 'Colour
    in the Picturesque' (article), 108;
    'Fully Licensed'(article), 98, 102–3;
    'Shops' (article), 101–2; 'Warmth in
    the West' (article), 102; *see also*
    Berkshire; *Buckinghamshire*;
    Lancashire (*Murray's Guides*);
    Oxon; *Shropshire*; *Wiltshire* (*Shell
    Guides*)
Piper, Myfanwy, 97, 150
Pitt-Rivers, Michael, 122
Plymouth, 66
Pope, Alexander: Twickenham garden,
    108
Portsea: St John's church, 48
Port Sunlight, 129–30
'Pot Pourri from a Surrey Garden' (JB;
    poem), 11
Powers, Alan, 50
Pre-Raphaelites, 144
Preston, Lancashire, 44
Price, Uvedale, 100, 109, 140, 146
Private Eye (magazine), 157
Protestantism: JB extols, 47–8
Pugin, Augustus Welby Northmore,
    41–2, 82

Quakers (Society of Friends): JB's
    membership of, 16–19, 46, 49,
    89–90; and Voysey's architecture, 41
Quennell, C. H. B. and (Sir) Peter, 57,
    73

Rayner, John, 57, 64, 73
Redding, Cyrus, 60–1

Rees, Vyvyan, 122
Regan, Maurice, 55–6
Reith Lectures (1955): NP delivers,
    138–45
Renaudot, Lucie, 22
Renoir, Auguste, 86, 128
'Return of Historicism, The' (NP;
    article), 158, 160
RIBA Journal, 158
'Richard Norman Shaw' (NP; article),
    1–6
Richards, (Sir) James M. ('Marx'), 83,
    93, 95, 99, 127, 148–9
Richardson, Sir Albert Edward, 10
Rochester Cathedral, 65, 68
Rochester, John Wilmot, 2nd Earl of, 155
Rococo style, 47
Roehampton: Alton Estate, 108
Rogers, Sir Richard, 168
Rosse, Anne Parsons, Countess of (*née*
    Messel), 147–8
Rossetti, Dante Gabriel, 144
Rousseau, Henri ('Douanier'), 87
Rowse, Alfred Leslie, 145
Royal Horticultural Hall, London, 23,
    32
Rudolph, Paul, 167
Ruskin, John, 80, 82
Russell, Gordon, 79–80, 93–4
Russell-Hitchcock, Henry, 100

'Sack of Bath' (JB; poem), 52
St Cyprian's church *see* Marylebone
St Enodoc, Cornwall, 6, 169
St James's Gazette, 130
St Pancras Hotel and railway station,
    London, 41, 149–50
St Paul's Cathedral, London: precincts,
    132–3, 146
Salisbury Cathedral, 71, 120
Sambourne, Linley, 147
Santini, Giovanni, 144
Sargent, Miles, 68
Saxon architecture, 48–9, 127–8
Scarfe, Norman, 122
Schapire, Miss: researches for NP, 112

Index